Acting on the Good News

Acting on the Good News

by
John MacArthur, Jr.

MOODY PRESS
CHICAGO

© 1987 by
JOHN F. MACARTHUR, JR.

All Scripture quotations, unless noted otherwise, are from the *New Scofield Reference Bible*, King James Version. Copyright © 1967 by Oxford University Press, Inc. Reprinted by permission.

Library of Congress Cataloging in Publication Data

MacArthur, John F.
    Acting on the good news.

    (John MacArthur's Bible studies)
    Includes index.
    1. Bible. N.T. Romans I, 1-16 —Criticism, interpre-
tation, etc. I. Title. II. Series: MacArthur, John F.
Bible studies.
BS2665.2.M175   1987   227'.106   86-31230
ISBN 0-8024-5348-1

1 2 3 4 5 6 7 Printing/LC/Year 91 90 89 88 87

Printed in the United States of America

Contents

These Bible studies are taken from messages delivered by Pastor-Teacher John MacArthur, Jr., at Grace Community Church in Panorama City, California. The recorded messages themselves may be purchased as a series or individually. Please request the current price list by writing to:

WORD OF GRACE COMMUNICATIONS
P.O. Box 4000
Panorama City, CA 91412

Or call the following number:
818-982-7000

1

The Preacher of the Good News

Outline

Introduction
A. The Bad News
   1. Selfishness
   2. Guilt
   3. Meaninglessness
   4. Hopelessness
B. The Good News
   1. Its significance
   2. Its source

Lesson
I. The Preacher of the Good News (v. 1)
   A. Paul—A Servant of Jesus Christ (v. 1*a*)
      1. A slave of dignity
      2. A slave of humility
         a) 1 Corinthians 3:5
         b) 1 Corinthians 4:1
   B. Paul—An Apostle of Jesus Christ (v. 1*b*)
      1. The calling
         a) Acts 9:15
         b) Acts 22:14-15
         c) Acts 26:16-17
         d) 1 Corinthians 9:16
         e) Galatians 1:1
      2. The concept
      3. The credentials
         a) The office of an apostle
         b) The origin of an apostle
         c) The signs of an apostle

C. Paul—Set Apart by Jesus Christ (v. 1c)
   1. The meaning of separation in the Old Testament
      a) Numbers 15:20
      b) Numbers 8:11
      c) Leviticus 20:26
   2. The meaning of separation in the New Testament
      a) Galatians 1:15
      b) Acts 13:2
      c) 2 Timothy 2:15

Conclusion

Introduction

A. The Bad News

A quick look at any newspaper or magazine shows that the world is getting worse and worse. The bad news that occurs on a large scale is only the multiplication of what occurs on an individual level. The term *bad news* has become a colloquialism to describe our era.

The reason there is so much bad news today is that people are in the grasp of a terrifying power that grips them deep inside. It causes men to self-destruct. That power is sin. There are four ways in which sin produces bad news.

1. Selfishness

It is truly bad news when everyone is bent on fulfilling his own desires at any price. The basic element in selfishness is the dominance of one's own ego above others. Satan displayed the epitome of selfishness when he said, "I will ascend into heaven, I will exalt my throne above the stars of God; I will sit also upon the mount of the congregation, in the sides of the north, I will ascend above the heights of the clouds, I will be like the most high" (Isa. 14:13-14). Man has inherited the propensity to sin and is utterly self-centered. Man will attempt whatever evil a society permits. He will go as far as society will tolerate. Man will consume everything based

Look up

8

on his own lust—things, people, and ultimately himself. Many times when a friend, spouse, or family member ceases to provide what an individual wants, he or she is discarded.

The sinful man's ultimate goal is to achieve self-satisfaction. Whether it is in business or marriage, man perverts everything because of his selfish lust for fame, dominance, popularity, money, and physical fulfillment. Sin pushes humanity to self-consumption. Someone has well said we ought to use things and love people, but instead we love things and use people. The end result of man's selfishness is that he is unable to have meaningful relationships. He is unwilling to give, and thus he forfeits that which is the truest source of joy—an unselfish, sacrificial love for others. Man becomes dominated by selfish greed, which alienates him from everyone and everything. He finally comes to a place of utter loneliness and despair. When man follows his own lust, he begins to realize the law of diminishing returns—the more he gets, the less it satisfies.

2. Guilt

Using and abusing people—or doing whatever else is necessary to indulge yourself—brings about guilt. God has designed man to feel sorrow when he sins; otherwise man could never recognize his need of God. Guilt is like pain. God has given us pain to tell us that we are sick or injured. Likewise, God has given us guilt to tell us that we are sinful and that something needs to change. The bad news is that man lives with anxiety, fear, psychological problems, ulcers, and myriad illnesses caused by his guilt. He may try to alleviate his guilt by drunkenness, debauchery, or even suicide. Man tries to cover his guilt with a frivolous facade. Some people try to rationalize away their guilt with money, possessions, alcohol, drugs, sex, travel, or psychoanalysis. Some blame their guilt on society, perhaps on a so-called antiquated biblical tradition. People will push off their sin on anything. But we only end up compounding our guilt when we blame someone else for it.

3. Meaninglessness

When man experiences selfishness and guilt, he will invariably ask himself, *Is what I'm experiencing all there is to life? What are the real answers? The real questions? Why am I alive? What is the real meaning of life?* Man is fed a steady diet of lies by Satan, who runs the world's evil system. And since his lies never really answer the question of man's existence, man is left with no answers. Edna St. Vincent Millay said this in her poem "Lament": "Life must go on; I forget just why." Many live in a series of twenty-four-hour periods without real significance, where little changes. The epitome of man's problem is summed up by Roquentin, the main character in philosopher Jean Paul Sartre's novel *Nausea*, who said, "I decided to kill myself to remove at least one superfluous life."

4. Hopelessness

Born out of the trauma and anxiety of meaninglessness is the realization that you have nothing to live for and nothing to look forward to. The only result of a self-centered, guilt-ridden, meaningless life is the starkness of death. That is why people mask the reality of death by laughing at it or ignoring it. They try to avoid the inevitable hopelessness—the sense there is nothing in this life or in the life to come—which is the worst news of all.

Thousands of babies are born every day into a world filled with bad news. With each passing day, men find themselves falling deeper into the human dilemma because they live in a world dominated by the father of lies—Satan himself. As a result, sin produces bad news. And even the small amounts of good news are but moments of rest in an unending saga of bad news. The periods of good news are like many peace treaties—those moments when everyone stops to reload. In between the bad news, much of the good news is short-lived.

B. The Good News

With so much bad news, can there really be any good news? Yes. The good news is that sin can be dealt with.

You don't have to be selfish. Guilt and anxiety can be alleviated. There is meaning to life and hope of life after death. The apostle Paul says in Romans 1:1 that the good news is the gospel, which is the good news of God. That is what the book of Romans is all about. Paul begins this epistle with the good news of God and ends with it as well (cf. 15:16). Bracketing the entire epistle is the great reality that there is good news from God.

1. Its significance

Paul called the gospel by many different phrases, but whatever he called it, it was good news. It is good news that man's sin can be forgiven, his guilt can be removed, his life can have meaning, and a hopeful future can be a reality.

Paul endeavors throughout the book of Romans to unfold the incomprehensible riches of the good news to man. But did you know that the entire thrust of all sixteen chapters of Romans is distilled into the first seven verses? Paul is so thrilled by what he wants to say that he can't wait to say it. He capsulizes his foundational thoughts in Romans 1:1-7. It is as if the seed of the gospel is in the first seven verses and then fully blooms throughout the rest of the epistle.

2. Its source

The Greek word for "gospel" in verse 1 is *euangelion*. It is used over sixty times by Paul in his epistles. Paul had lived all his life hearing only the bad news, but once he heard the good news he couldn't help but tell everyone about it. Tyndale wrote that the word *euangelion* signifies good, merry, glad, and joyful tidings that makes a man's heart rejoice and makes him sing and dance and leap for joy. The merry, glad, and joyful news is that God will deliver us from our sin.

The thrust of the Greek text of Romans 1:1 is that the good news is from God. It is important that Paul distinguished between ordinary good news and good news from God because *euangelion* was a common Greek word. In one of its more prominent occurrences, it was

11

used to precede messages to the people from the emperor. In the Roman Empire, the people were required to worship the emperor as if he were a god. Whenever someone from the emperor's official party made an important announcement, it was called *euangelion*, or good news. The messenger would proclaim, "Good news, the emperor has given birth to an heir" or "Good news, a new emperor has acceded to the throne."

Paul in effect says, "I'm writing to you at Rome who are used to hearing the *euangelion* of the empire, and I'm telling you I've got good news—not from Caesar but from God." The good news is from God. God brings good news to those who are undeserving.

The Way God Loves

Dr. Donald Grey Barnhouse illustrated the Christian's unworthiness by recounting this story:

"It was told that a young man, much loved of his mother, pursued a wicked course that took him deeper and deeper into sin. He became enamored of an evil woman who dragged him further and further into unrighteousness. The mother naturally sought to draw him back to a higher plane, and the other woman resented it bitterly. One night, the story goes, the evil woman chided the man with an accusation that he did not really love her. He vowed that he did. She appealed to his drunken mind, saying that if he loved her he would rid them of his mother and her pleadings. According to the story, the young man rushed from the room to the nearby house in which his mother dwelt, and dealt her death blows, tearing the heart from her body to carry it back to his paramour. Then comes the climax of the tale. As he rushed on in his insane folly, he stumbled and fell, and from the bleeding heart there came a voice, 'My son, are you hurt?' That's the way God loves you" (*Expositions of Bible Doctrines Taking the Epistle to the Romans as a Point of Departure,* vol. 1 [Grand Rapids: Eerdmans, 1952], pp. 21-22).

Charles Wesley put the same thought into his hymn "Depth of Mercy":

> Depth of mercy! can there be
> Mercy still reserved for me?
> Can my God His wrath forbear—
> Me, the chief of sinners, spare?
>
> I have long withstood His grace,
> Long provoked Him to His face,
> Would not hearken to His calls,
> Grieved Him by a thousand falls.

Wesley marveled at the good news from God to undeserving men.

Lesson

I. THE PREACHER OF THE GOOD NEWS (v. 1)

"Paul, a servant of Jesus Christ, called to be an apostle, separated unto the gospel of God."

God called a unique man, Paul, to be a major spokesman for the good news. God had committed to him mysteries concerning the church that had been hidden from past generations but were now to be revealed (cf. Eph. 3:3; Col. 1:26-27). Paul was God's keynote speaker for the heralding of the good news to the Gentiles. He had a remarkable Jewish heritage, Greek education, and Roman citizenship. He had incredible abilities as a leader, fighter, motivator, and articulator who was specially called and converted by God Himself. From Jerusalem to Macedonia, Paul had completed three missionary journeys proclaiming the good news. And even though Paul was mightily gifted by God and could perform miracles, he could not rid himself of his own thorn in the flesh (2 Cor. 12:7-9). Paul could cause prisons to fall (Acts 16:26) yet became a permanent prisoner. All the preachers who have ever preached since Paul have depended on his sermons for their material. Paul left a great legacy of biblical teaching through the inspiration of the Holy Spirit.

A. Paul—A Servant of Jesus Christ (v. 1a)

"Paul, a servant of Jesus Christ."

1. A slave of dignity

The Greek word used here for servant is *doulos*, which means "slave." Those who love the Lord are His servants.

a) Exodus 21:5-6—The Lord said, "If the servant shall plainly say, I love my master, my wife, and my children, I will not go out free; then his master shall bring him unto the judges. He shall also bring him to the door, or unto the door post; and his master shall bore his ear through with an awl, and he shall serve him forever." Because of his love for his master, this servant became known as a bond slave. He didn't serve because he was forced to but because he wanted to. He became a slave of love.

b) Genesis 26:24—"The Lord appeared unto him [Isaac] the same night, and said, I am the God of Abraham, thy father: fear not, for I am with thee, and will bless thee, and multiply thy seed for my *servant* Abraham's sake" (emphasis added).

c) Numbers 12:7—The Lord said, "My *servant*, Moses, is faithful in all mine house" (emphasis added).

d) Joshua 24:29—Scripture says, "It came to pass . . . that Joshua, the son of Nun, the *servant* of the Lord, died, being an hundred and ten years old" (emphasis added).

e) 2 Samuel 7:5—The Lord said, "Go and tell my *servant*, David, Thus saith the Lord, Shalt thou build me an house for me to dwell in" (emphasis added).

f) Isaiah 20:3—"The Lord said . . . my *servant*, Isaiah, hath walked naked and barefoot three years for a sign and wonder upon Egypt and upon Ethiopia" (emphasis added).

14

g) Isaiah 53:11—The Lord prophesied about the coming Messiah by saying, "He shall see of the travail of his soul, and shall be satisfied; by his knowledge shall my righteous *servant* justify many; for he shall bear their iniquities" (emphasis added).

Paul was a bond slave. It was something he chose out of love, not fear. There were perhaps millions of slaves in the Roman Empire. For the most part, they were treated not as persons but as objects. If a master wanted to kill his slaves, he could. Some Bible commentators think Paul is using *doulos* only in its Jewish sense—not in the Roman sense—and is thereby affirming love for Christ. The Hebrew concept of servant could include someone in the highest ranks of service. Kings had servants, and in that sense, a servant could be someone who had great honor and dignity.

2. A slave of humility

However, to see Paul as referring to his slavery to Christ only out of love does not encompass the entire point. There is a certain incomprehensible dignity in being called a servant of Jesus Christ. But it is not correct to disregard the Gentile understanding of the term. The Greek term itself (*doulos*) referred to abject slavery—a term of humility, not dignity. Paul used two other words to speak of his servitude.

a) 1 Corinthians 3:5—"Who, then, is Paul, and who is Apollos, but ministers by whom ye believed, even as the Lord gave to every man?" The Greek word for "ministers" is *diakonos,* which means "table waiter." Paul described himself as nothing more than a menial servant for Christ.

b) 1 Corinthians 4:1—"Let a man so account of us, as of the ministers of Christ." Here the Greek word translated "ministers" is *hupēretes.* The prefix of the word, *huper,* means "under," and the suffix, *etes,* comes from a word that means "to row." A trireme ship had three levels of oars with three levels of galley slaves who rowed it. Paul was saying he was a third-level galley slave for Christ.

15

Combined in the term *slave* is the Hebrew concept of dignity, honor, and respect, but also the Greek concept of humility. Paul paradoxically finds himself both exalted as the servant of Christ and debased as well. That is the ambivalence every representative of Jesus Christ must face.

When I think of the honor in being a preacher of the gospel of Jesus Christ, it sometimes overwhelms me. There is no higher calling in life than to proclaim the gospel of God from the pulpit and to be able to teach the Word of God under the power of the Holy Spirit. Yet there is also a paradox that requires the minister of Christ to realize he has absolutely no right to think he deserves to minister. He must have the proper perspective of being an unworthy slave who has the incomprehensible privilege of proclaiming the good news.

B. Paul—An Apostle of Jesus Christ (v. 1*b*)

"Called to be an apostle."

1. The calling

The best rendering of the Greek text of Romans 1:1 is that Paul was a called apostle. His apostleship was not based on his own decision. God effectually called him to that office. It was not a human appointment. The term *apostle* was first used by the Lord in Luke 6:13. He referred to the twelve as His apostles. Paul was also called an apostle by God Himself.

a) Acts 9:15—The Lord said of Paul, "He is a chosen vessel unto me, to bear my name before the Gentiles, and kings, and the children of Israel." Paul was on his way to Damascus to persecute Christians, but the Lord stopped him dead in his tracks. The decision for Paul to preach did not originate with him; it was God's sovereign choice.

b) Acts 22:14-15—Recounting his conversion, Paul quoted Ananias as saying, "The God of our fathers hath chosen thee, that thou shouldest know his will, and see that Just One, and shouldest hear the voice of his mouth. For thou shalt be his witness unto all men of what thou hast seen and heard."

c) Acts 26:16-17—The Lord had said to Paul, "Rise, and stand upon thy feet; for I have appeared unto thee for this purpose, to make thee a minister and a witness both of these things which thou hast seen, and of those things in which I will appear unto thee." Paul obeyed the heavenly vision given by God on the Damascus Road. He was called of God to be an apostle.

d) 1 Corinthians 9:16—Paul affirmed his call to the ministry by saying, "Though I preach the gospel, I have nothing to glory of; for necessity is laid upon me; yea, woe is unto me, if I preach not the gospel!"

e) Galatians 1:1—Paul began the epistle to the Galatians this way: "Paul, an apostle (not of men, neither by man, but by Jesus Christ, and God the Father, who raised him from the dead)." Later in verse 12 he says, "I neither received it [the gospel] of man, neither was I taught it, but by the revelation of Jesus Christ." Paul's call to the ministry was from Christ Himself.

2. The concept

The Greek word for apostle is *apŏstolos*, which means "one who is sent, commissioned, or dispatched." It refers to a messenger, ambassador, or an envoy. There were certain vessels referred to as "apostolic boats." They were common cargo ships. The word *apostle* meant anyone or anything dispatched or sent. Paul was saying he had been sent by Jesus Christ Himself. The term *apostle* itself appears over seventy-eight times in the New Testament, the majority of those references being used to describe the twelve disciples and Paul. They were specially sent by Christ.

There is a story of an old black preacher who pastored a small country church. He always preached his heart out because he was a humble and godly man. A young man came to preach one Sunday night at his church. He was cocky, self-assured, and thought he was more than the

17

people deserved. As he preached, it was apparent that his attitude was not one of love or compassion. When he finished preaching, the old black preacher came up to him and said, "Young man, was you sent or did you just went?" There are probably many other preachers who are in the latter category. The apostle Paul was sent. He knew that because God had affirmed it to him.

3. The credentials

a) The office of an apostle

There is also an official sense in which the word *apostle* must be understood. An apostle was someone who held an official office within the church. The term can have a broad meaning to describe all who bear the message of Christ. All Christians are sent by Christ into the world to preach the gospel (cf. Matt. 28:18-20). But the ones who were specially sent by Christ bear the title *apostle*.

b) The origin of an apostle

The New Testament describes various people as apostles in addition to the twelve and Paul. But they did not hold the specific office of an apostle. To be in the office of apostle, you would have to have been verbally called by Jesus Christ into the ministry and to have been eye witnesses of Christ and His resurrection. Paul qualified because he saw Christ on the Damascus Road. The apostles and their close associates were also to be the human authors of the New Testament because Jesus made the promise to them that the Spirit would come and bring to their remembrance all that He had said to them (cf. John 14:26).

The twelve apostles (Matthias replacing Judas) and Paul were called by Jesus Himself. The Lord said through the prophet Jeremiah, "Woe be unto the shepherds who destroy and scatter the sheep of my pasture!" (Jer. 23:1). The church today is filled with preachers who are talking but should not be listened to. They do not have the anointing of God on them and have corrupted the church throughout the centuries.

   c) The signs of an apostle

   The apostles were given the ability to do signs, wonders, and miracles, which Paul calls the signs of an apostle (2 Cor. 12:12). Their office was not restricted to a local church or for a certain period of time in their lives. Once you were an apostle, you were an apostle for life. They became the foundation on which all the history of the church is built.

C. Paul—Set Apart by Jesus Christ (v. 1c)

"Separated unto the gospel of God."

1. The meaning of separation in the Old Testament

   You cannot serve God unless you are separated. The word has the idea of being set apart for a specific task or purpose.

   a) Numbers 15:20—The Lord said to Moses, "Ye shall offer up a cake of the first of your dough for an heave offering." God wanted the firstfruits of the land to be set apart to honor Him.

   b) Numbers 8:11—Again the Lord said to Moses, "Aaron shall offer the Levites before the Lord for an offering of the children of Israel, that they may execute the service of the Lord." God desired to set apart the best men by consecrating the Levites to His service.

   c) Leviticus 20:26—The Lord said, "Ye shall be holy unto me; for I, the Lord, am holy, and have separated you from other people, that ye should be mine." God took the whole nation of Israel and separated them from all other nations for His glory.

   In each of those passages, the Septuagint—the Greek version of the Old Testament—uses a form of the word *aphōrizein*, which is the same word used in Romans 1:1.

It refers to separation in the fullest sense. Paul knew that once he was called as an apostle, he would be disconnected from his past. In the middle of *aphōrizein* is *phoriz*, which may refer to the word *Pharisee* meaning "separated one." Paul had been the most ardent Pharisee, separated unto the traditions of the Jewish people (Phil. 3:5). In a sense he could say, "I am a Pharisee separated unto the gospel of God."

2. The meaning of separation in the New Testament

   a) Galatians 1:15—Paul said, "It pleased God, who separated me from my mother's womb, and called me by his grace." Paul was elected by God unto the gospel of God.

   b) Acts 13:2—The Holy Spirit said to the church at Antioch, "Separate me Barnabas and Saul for the work unto which I have called them." The secret of Paul's service was that he was a bond slave of Christ, utterly surrendered to the Lord. He was sent to carry the message of the cross, so he cut the cord with the world. There are so many people in the gospel ministry who see little fruit and no power because they are unwilling to be separated from the world.

   c) 2 Timothy 2:15—Paul said to Timothy, "Study to show thyself approved unto God, a workman that needeth not to be ashamed, rightly dividing the word of truth." Timothy had come to the point in his life where his ministry was falling apart. In verse 6 of chapter 1 Paul tells Timothy to make use of the gift he has for preaching and teaching, which has been confirmed by the laying on of Paul's hands. Timothy had been getting lazy in the ministry.

   He had also become timid (1:7). He had been personally discipled by Paul and was gifted enough to have followed Paul as the pastor of the Ephesian church. Paul had even said to the Corinthians, "I sent unto you Timothy, who is my beloved son and faithful in the Lord, who shall bring you into remembrance of my ways which are in Christ" (1 Cor. 4:17). He may have been involved in the "profane and vain babblings" of speculative philosophy (2:16). Verses 22-23 of the same chapter indicate he was getting embroiled in youthful lusts as well as striving in "foolish and unlearned questions."

Timothy had been influenced by the world's evil system. Paul was exhorting Timothy not to be caught up in the lusts of this world. When you are called into the ministry of Jesus Christ, you must sever your ties with the world.

Conclusion

Paul was not only a servant of Christ but also called as an apostle and separated to God in holiness. He didn't get himself entangled with the affairs of this life (2 Tim. 2:4). Many men today have left the ministry because they love money or possessions. They couldn't sever the ties with the world, so they fell into sin. Some men are concerned most about their reputation before men; so when they get an opportunity to speak, they make sure they never offend anyone. But in so doing, they offend God (cf. John 12:42-43).

Paul was a man after God's own heart. Romans 1:1 says it all: his position—"servant"; his authority—"called to be an apostle by God"; his power—"separated"; his message—"the gospel [good news] from God."

Focusing on the Facts

1. Why is there so much bad news today (see p. 8)?
2. The basic element in selfishness is the dominance of your own _____ above others (see p. 8).
3. True or False: The ultimate goal in life for sinful man is to achieve self-satisfaction (see p. 9).
4. What is the law of diminishing returns, and how does it affect man's attitudes (see p. 9)?
5. What is the second area of bad news in today's world, and what is its result (see p. 9)?

6. Explain the bad news of meaninglessness and hopelessness (see p. 10).
7. What is the good news? Explain how it relates to selfishness, guilt, meaninglessness, and hopelessness (see pp. 10-11).
8. What is the significance of the first seven verses in Romans (see p. 11)?
9. What was the secular understanding of good news? What is Paul's contrast (see pp. 11-12)?
10. In what ways was Paul blessed to preach the mysteries concerning the church (p. 13)?
11. Explain the Hebrew and Greek concepts concerning slaves. How did Paul exhibit both characteristics (see pp. 14-15)?
12. A minister must have the proper perspective of being an _____ _____ who also has the incomprehensible _____ of proclaiming the good news (see p. 16).
13. Explain how Paul was called to be an apostle (see pp. 16-17).
14. According to the criteria for the office of an apostle, can there be any apostles in the church today? Explain your answer from Scripture (see p. 18).
15. When you are called into the ministry of Jesus Christ, you must _____ your ties with the world (see p. 21).

Pondering the Principles

1. The apostle Paul was a servant of Jesus Christ. He recognized the dignity of the position but also knew of its humility. Every Christian is likewise called to be a servant of Christ. That involves serving others. Do you have a servant's heart? Do you desire to please God by serving your fellow man? Read the following verses and ask God to make you into a Christlike servant: John 12:26, 13:14-16, and 2 Corinthians 4:5.

2. Paul realized that to be a proclaimer of the gospel, he had to separate himself from evil men. Men will not listen to the message of Christ if the one presenting it is living in an unrighteous manner. Are you separating yourself from evil so that the gospel is not being discredited because of you? If there is anything in your life that is discrediting the gospel, confess your sin to God and ask Him to make you holy on a daily basis. Memorize Hebrews 12:14: "Holiness, without which no man shall see the Lord."

2

The Promise and Person
of the Good News

Outline

Introduction
A. The Search
B. The Seduction
   1. Man's longing
   2. Man's lostness
C. The Solution
   1. The descriptions of the good news
   2. The dimensions of the good news
      a) 1 Corinthians 2:2
      b) 1 Corinthians 9:22-23
   3. The declaration of the good news
      a) Greater than the greatest philosophers
      b) Greater than the greatest painters
      c) Greater than the greatest poets
      d) Greater than the greatest musicians
D. The Simplicity
   1. Of the gospel
   2. Of the Lord's prayer

Review
I. The Preacher of the Good News (v. 1)
   A. Paul—A Servant of Jesus Christ
   B. Paul—An Apostle of Jesus Christ
   C. Paul—Set Apart by Jesus Christ

Lesson

II. The Promise of the Good News (v. 2)
  A. The Continuity of the Gospel
      1. The accusations against Paul
      2. The accusations against Jesus
          a) Matthew 5:21-22
          b) Matthew 5:17
  B. The Consistency of the Gospel
      1. The manner
      2. The means
  C. The Character of the Gospel
      1. It is not of human origin
          a) John 5:39
          b) Luke 24:25-27
          c) Hebrews 10:7
      2. It is of divine origin
          a) Romans 7:12
          b) 2 Peter 1:20-21
III. The Person of the Good News (vv. 3-4)
  A. His Name
      1. Jesus
      2. Christ
      3. Lord
          a) Romans 9:5
          b) Philippians 2:6
          c) Colossians 2:9
  B. His Sonship
      1. His eternal rank
      2. His incarnate role
          a) Hebrews 1:5
          b) 2 Samuel 7:14
          c) Philippians 2:6-8
          d) John 17:4
          e) John 1:1
  C. His Birth
      1. Jesus became a man
      2. Jesus sympathizes with us
      3. Jesus was born of the house of David
  D. His Resurrection
      1. The declaration of His sonship (v. 4*a*)
          a) The boundary
          b) The beauty

Introduction

A. The Search

Man's eternal soul is made in such a way that it knows no rest until it finds its rest in God. Socrates said, "O that someone would arise to show us God." Socrates was simply articulating the hunger that is in every human heart for God. Pascal said in his *Pensées*, "In every man there is a God-shaped vacuum." There is no greater example of this hunger of God than the proliferation of religious systems throughout the history of mankind. The issue isn't *whether* man will worship, but *what* he will worship. Unfortunately, in the bent of his perverse nature, man inevitably rejects the true God and forms gods of his own making. But such gods provide no solution to man's sinful condition.

B. The Seduction

Man's sinfulness presents a basic problem. How can he escape from his condition? Man's world could be represented by a small box or cube that is closed on all sides. He exists in a time-space dimension outside the supernatural realm. God is outside man's world. Man speculates about what's on the outside and searches to know if there is really something outside his box. It is impossible for him to escape the box because by its very definition, the natural cannot enter into the supernatural. That which is confined to time and space cannot escape into eternity and infinity.

1. Man's longing

Because there is something within man that longs to comprehend what is outside the box, he invents deities that he thinks are there. That is the reason we have such a proliferation of religions in the world, not to mention the inexhaustive interest in space travel and extraterrestrial beings. They are an extension of man's desire to escape his box. Many religions say, "Be a good person, and you'll discover God. Just be sure that you fulfill certain routines and rituals, and you'll meet God."

2. Man's lostness

Man's longing to transcend the box cannot be overcome because he is confined to the box by his very nature. No one, no matter what we are led to believe, can go into a phone booth and come out Superman.

C. The Solution

Christ is the only way man can ever hope to leave his box. Christianity acknowledges that man can't get out of his box but says the good news is that God has invaded the box. He has entered into man's world to tell him he can dwell with God forever. The good news of Christianity is that since man couldn't get out of his box, God came into the box. The natural cannot ascend to the supernatural, but the supernatural can condescend to the natural.

1. The descriptions of the good news

The good news Paul speaks of in Romans 1:1 is the good news that God has burst through the box and desires to communicate with man. In a world filled with bad news, it is remarkable to know that God Himself has given us good news. That is especially true when you realize that man is utterly unworthy of any good news. Yet in spite of that the apostle Paul reiterates again and again that the good news comes from God.

a) 1 Timothy 1:11—Paul said, "According to the glorious gospel of the blessed God, which was committed to my trust."

b) Romans 15:29—Paul also said, "I am sure that, when I come unto you, I shall come in the fullness of the blessing of the gospel of Christ."

c) Acts 20:24—Paul said, "The ministry, which I have received of the Lord Jesus, to testify the gospel of the grace of God."

d) Romans 10:15—Paul said, "How beautiful are the feet of them that preach the gospel of peace, and bring glad tidings of good things!"

e) Ephesians 1:13—Paul also said, "In whom ye also trusted, after ye heard the word of truth, the gospel of your salvation."

f) Romans 1:1—Paul said he was "separated unto the gospel of God."

g) Romans 1:9—Paul followed his description of the gospel in verse 1 by saying, "God is my witness, whom I serve with my spirit in the gospel of his Son."

h) Romans 1:16—Paul firmly stated, "I am not ashamed of the gospel of Christ; for it is the power of God unto salvation."

2. The dimensions of the good news

The apostle Paul used different terms to emphasize different aspects of the good news. He speaks in Romans 2:16 of "the day when God shall judge the secrets of men by Jesus Christ according to my gospel." He used a possessive pronoun to explain that the gospel of Christ came into his possession by his faith in Christ and that it was his gospel to preach (cf. Rom. 16:25). The entire thrust of Paul's ministry was to preach the good news about Christ.

a) 1 Corinthians 2:2—Paul said, "I determined not to know any thing among you, except Jesus Christ, and him crucified."

b) 1 Corinthians 9:22-23—Paul also said, "I am made all things to all men, that I might by all means save some. And this I do for the gospel's sake."

God has come into man's world to tell him what He Himself is like and to tell man how he can know God. Jesus Christ is the good news that invaded the box to reveal God to man.

3. The declaration of the good news

Jesus Christ is the most incomparable personality of all human history. Believers and unbelievers alike have recognized Christ's greatness. The difference for the unbeliever is that he does not surrender to Him as Lord.

a) Greater than the greatest philosophers

Socrates taught for 40 years, Plato for 50 years, and Aristotle for 40 years. Jesus's public ministry lasted less than three years, yet the influence of His life far outweighs the combined 130 years of the three greatest philosophers of all antiquity.

b) Greater than the greatest painters

Jesus never painted a picture, yet some of the finest paintings of Raphael, Michelangelo, da Vinci, and many other artists found their inspiration in Christ.

c) Greater than the greatest poets

Jesus wrote no poetry, but Dante, Milton, and scores of the world's greatest poets have been inspired by Christ as by no other. Ralph Waldo Emerson said that the name of Jesus "is not so much written as ploughed into the history of this world" (*The Collected Works of Ralph Waldo Emerson*, vol. 1 [Cambridge, Mass.: Harvard, 1971], p. 80).

d) Greater than the greatest musicians

Jesus wrote no music, and yet Haydn, Handel, Beethoven, Bach, Mendelssohn, and myriad others reached their highest perfection in compositions about Him.

Jesus has affected our society like no other. The incomparable Christ is the good news. And what makes it such good news is that man is so undeserving. That we don't deserve the good news makes it all the more true that God is gracious.

D. The Simplicity

It is thrilling to read Romans 1:1-7 and see the infinite mind of God, who in a few words condenses the essence of the unfathomable gospel, covering everything from the incarnation of Christ to living the Christian life.

1. Of the gospel

Only 297 English words are required to sum up all of God's oral law in the Ten Commandments. God distilled it even more when He said, "Thou shalt love the Lord, thy God, with all thy heart, and with all thy soul, and with all thy mind. This is the first and great commandment. And the second is like it, thou shalt love thy neighbor as thyself" (Matt. 22:37-40).

2. Of the Lord's prayer

The definitive teaching on prayer is the Lord's Prayer in Matthew 6:9-13, which is only sixty-five words. Man doesn't have that capacity for essential brevity. One governmental study on regulating the price of cabbage ran over twenty-six thousand words!

Review

I. THE PREACHER OF THE GOOD NEWS (v. 1; see pp. 13-21)

A. Paul—A Servant of Jesus Christ (see pp. 14-16)

B. Paul—An Apostle of Jesus Christ (see pp. 16-19)

C. Paul—Set Apart by Jesus Christ (see pp. 19-21)

Lesson

II. THE PROMISE OF THE GOOD NEWS (v. 2)

"Which [the gospel] he had promised before by his prophets in the holy scriptures."

A. The Continuity of the Gospel

Paul begins his discussion of the gospel in verse 2 by saying, "Which he [God] had promised before by his prophets." He is saying that the good news is not something new. It is not out of continuity with the rest of Scripture. It isn't simply a novel idea or a change in God's strategy. It was promised long ago.

1. The accusations against Paul

Some were saying that the gospel was some revolutionary new message that was in no way connected to traditional Judaism. The apostle Paul himself was accused of being anti-Jewish. A sect known as the Judaizers condemned Paul and his message because they said he spoke against Moses, the law of God, and the Temple. They accused him of taking Gentiles into the inner Temple, where they were forbidden to go (Acts 21:27-29). So Paul—wanting to set the record straight—said the good news of God was nothing new, for it was indicated in the promises of the prophets who wrote in holy Scripture. There are at least 330 prophecies in the Old Testament that were fulfilled in Christ's first coming. The Old Testament laid the foundation for the coming of the New Testament gospel.

2. The accusations against Jesus

Jesus faced the same accusations Paul did. He too was not in agreement with contemporary Jewish theology of His day (Matt. 15:1-3). He denied the Pharisees' so-called devotion because of its hypocrisy. Many in His day were saying, "Is what Jesus saying new truth? Is He really speaking for God? He doesn't say what the Pharisees say. He in fact, says the opposite of what we're taught."

30

a) Matthew 5:21-22—Jesus said, "Ye have heard that it was said by them of old, Thou shalt not kill and whosoever shall kill shall be in danger of judgment; but I say unto you that whosoever is angry with his brother without a cause shall be in danger of judgment." When Jesus said, "Ye have heard that it was said by them of old," He was saying, "Your tradition teaches you, but I say unto you. . . ." He then gave completely different instructions. The "ye have heard that it was said" statements were not part of the Old Testament but a perversion of Scripture by the Pharisees' tradition.

b) Matthew 5:17—Jesus said, "Think not that I am come to destroy the law, or the prophets; I am not come to destroy, but to fulfill." Jesus was not condemning Old Testament law, simply the tradition that had been built up around it. The religious leaders had so perverted the law of God that Jesus had to declare, "I say unto you that except your righteousness shall exceed the righteousness of the scribes and Pharisees, ye shall in no case enter into the kingdom of heaven" (v. 20).

B. The Consistency of the Gospel

The Old Testament is completely consistent with the New. The good news is old, not new. Some Jewish people say, "I can't become a Christian because I'm Jewish, and that would be denying my heritage." If you are Jewish and you haven't become a Christian, the truth is you have denied your heritage because you have denied the New Covenant of which the Hebrew Scriptures speak (Jer. 31:27-40; Ezek. 36:26-38). When Christ preached the good news of the kingdom, people wondered if He was a revolutionary. But He was simply exposing their heretical theology that destroyed the continuity between the Old and New Covenants.

1. The manner

Hebrews 1:1-2 says, "God, who at sundry times and in diverse manners spoke in time past unto the fathers by the prophets, hath in these last days spoken unto us by

31

his Son, whom he hath appointed heir of all things, by whom also he made the worlds." The writer is saying that God spoke by the prophets in the Old Testament and by His Son in the New.

2. The means

First Peter 1:10-11 says, "Of which salvation the prophets have inquired and searched diligently, who prophesied of the grace that should come unto you, searching what, or what manner of time the Spirit of Christ who was in them did signify, when he testified beforehand the sufferings of Christ, and the glory that should follow." The prophets themselves realized their writings were incomplete. The New Covenant clarified the gospel of Christ.

Every sacrificial lamb in the Old Testament spoke of the ultimate sacrifice—Jesus Christ. The Old Covenant spoke of the time when the Messiah would come, yet when the most incredible event of all history came to pass, the Jewish people killed the Messiah and denied that He had any correlation with the Hebrew Scriptures. That is why Paul said the good news of Jesus Christ is exactly what was promised in the Old Testament.

C. The Character of the Gospel

The phrase "by the prophets in the holy scriptures" in verse 2 refers to all the writers of Scripture. The Old Testament was commonly called "the law and the prophets." The Jewish people divided the Old Testament into those two general categories, although some would also single out "the writings." But basically the phrase "the prophets" would encompass everything but the law. The law was written by Moses, and he is called a prophet (Deut. 18:15). The term can encompass all of the writers of the Old Testament. The gospel was promised throughout holy Scripture.

1. It is not of human origin

The reason Paul spoke of Scripture in this way was to emphasize its origin. The Scriptures are holy and therefore not authored by men. They are set apart, divine, unique, righteous, and godly. People often ask me why we should believe the Bible is inspired. One good reason is that God says it is.

a) John 5:39—Jesus said, "Search the scriptures; for in them ye think ye have eternal life; and they are they which testify of me."

b) Luke 24:25-27—In speaking to the men on the road to Emmaus Jesus said, "O foolish ones, and slow of heart to believe in all that the prophets have spoken! Ought not Christ to have suffered these things, and to enter into his glory? And beginning at Moses and all the prophets, he expounded unto them, in all the scriptures, the things concerning himself."

c) Hebrews 10:7—Jesus said, "In the volume of the book it is written of me." The Old Testament is filled with the promise of the good news. Whether you go from Genesis to Malachi, or anywhere in between, you will find the revelation of Jesus Christ.

2. It is of divine origin

a) Romans 7:12—Paul said, "The law is holy, and the commandment holy, and just, and good." God's truth is pure.

b) 2 Peter 1:20-21—Peter said, "No prophecy of the scripture is of any private interpretation. For the prophecy came not at any time by the will of man, but holy men of God spoke as they were moved by the Holy Spirit."

III. THE PERSON OF THE GOOD NEWS (vv. 3-4)

"Concerning his Son, Jesus Christ our Lord, who was made of the seed of David according to the flesh, and declared to be the Son of God with power, according to the spirit of holiness, by the resurrection from the dead."

A. His Name

Romans 1:2 is actually a parenthetical statement introducing the thrust of Paul's explanation of the gospel in verses 3-4. It is the gospel of God concerning His Son, Jesus Christ our Lord.

1. Jesus

The name *Jesus* means "Savior." Matthew 1:21 says, "She [Mary] shall bring forth a son, and thou shalt call his name JESUS; for he shall save his people from their sins."

2. Christ

The title *Christ* means "anointed one." Jesus the Christ has been anointed by God as a King and Priest.

3. Lord

The designation *Lord* means "sovereign ruler."

a) Romans 9:5—Paul said, "As concerning the flesh, Christ came, who is over all, God blessed forever."

b) Philippians 2:6—Paul said that Christ, "Being in the form of God, thought it not robbery to be equal with God."

c) Colossians 2:9—Paul said, "In him [Christ] dwelleth all the fullness of the Godhead bodily."

B. His Sonship

1. His eternal rank

There is no question that Jesus Christ is God. He is Lord, yet He is also referred to as the Son of God. Many have asked how can He be both God and the Son of God.

2. His incarnate role

We must first determine in what sense Jesus is the Son of God. The term *Son* was used by Paul and the other New Testament writers to speak of Christ at His incarnation. Jesus became a Son in taking on the role of the Son of God at His incarnation. Over the years, theologians have debated about whether Christ is the Son of God in eternity. Christ is and always has been the second member of the Trinity but only became a Son in His incarnation.

When you think of the word *son* you probably think of the submission, obedience, and honor shown to one's father. That is the sense in which Jesus is the Son. Nowhere in Scripture does it say that Jesus has eternally been the Son. He is called "the angel of Jehovah" in the Old Testament when He came to earth to function as an angelic being. However, that doesn't mean He functioned eternally as an angel. Likewise, just because He took the role of a Son in His incarnation doesn't mean He had been eternally functioning as a Son to the Father. The term *Son*, then, refers only to Christ's incarnation.

The phrase "who was made" in verse 3 is from the Greek verb *ginomai* and could be translated "who became." It is a statement of transition from one state to another. Jesus did not come into existence when He was born. He has always existed. In the incarnation, He simply took the role of a Son. That is why the text doesn't say He was made or created at His incarnation. He "was made of the seed of David according to the flesh" (v. 3). He made the transition from His lofty position with God to the humiliating position of dwelling with sinful man as a man Himself in the role of the Son.

a) Hebrews 1:5—The writer of Hebrews here quotes Psalm 2:7: "Thou art my Son, this day have I begotten thee." That verse explains that there was a day in which the Second Person of the Trinity assumed the role of a Son. The rest of the verse says, "I will be to him a Father, and he shall be to me a Son." Both those verbs are in the future tense denoting that there will be a time when the First Person of the Trinity will act as a Father and the Second Person of the Trinity will be in the role of a Son.

b) 2 Samuel 7:14—God said this to David about the Messiah: "I will be his father, and he shall be my son." The Old Testament declares that God will one day have a Son. Jesus was always God and has eternally existed, but He also took on the title of *Son*.

c) Philippians 2:6-8—Paul said that Christ, "being in the form of God, thought it not robbery to be equal with God, but made himself of no reputation, and took upon him the form of a servant, and was made in the likeness of men; and, being found in fashion as a man, he humbled himself and became obedient unto death, even the death of the cross." There was no Father-Son relationship among the Trinity in eternity, rather there was complete equality. At the incarnation, Christ took on the role or function of a servant.

d) John 17:4—Jesus said, "I have finished the work which thou gavest me to do." That cannot refer to Christ's work in sustaining creation, because He will never cease from that (Heb. 1:3). What work was He alluding to? The work of the cross and His role as the Son.

e) John 1:1—John said, "In the beginning was the Word, and the Word was with God, and the Word was God." Verse 14 says, "The Word was made flesh and dwelt among us." Verse 1 describes His exalted, eternal state and verse 14 His humbled, human status as the Son.

C. His Birth

The phrase "of the seed of David according to the flesh" refers to the virgin birth of Christ. His mother Mary was in the line of David, as was Joseph. He had to be born into the family of David to be the true Messiah. This phrase talks about Jesus Christ—God in the flesh—coming to earth as a man.

1. Jesus became a man

The good news is that God became a man. He was born into a family. He was flesh and blood. He was born of a virgin but nonetheless born. He became a Son. Luke 2:11 says, "Unto you is born this day in the city of David a Savior, who is Christ the Lord."

Many might say, "What's the difference in Christ's being a Son eternally or becoming one at His incarnation?" The main reason is in the interest of biblical accuracy. Also, to see Christ as becoming a Son is to see the majesty of His condescension. He was not eternally subservient to God but eternally equal to God. The marvelous reality of His incarnation was that He stepped down from His majesty to become a son. But why?

2. Jesus sympathizes with us

One of the reasons Jesus left His place in heaven was to experience humanness and become our sympathetic high priest (Heb. 4:14-15). Jesus became a man to die for men. He was our substitute, bearing the brunt of God's wrath.

3. Jesus was born of the house of David

Jesus had to be a man to sympathize with us, but He wasn't just any man. Verse 3 says He was "of the seed of David." Jesus was born into the right family, thus falling in line with God's plan to rule and redeem the world. If He hadn't been the son of David, He couldn't have been the Messiah, because the Old Testament predicted the Messiah would come from David's lineage (2 Sam. 7:12-13; Ps. 89:3-4, 24; Isa. 11:1-5; Jer. 23:5-6; 33:14-16; Ezek. 34:23-24; 37:24).

Verses 27, 32-33, and 69 of Luke 1 all speak of Christ as being the Son of David. God became a man to sympathize with man and bear the sins of man. Christ is the right man because He is descended from the throne of David and has the right to rule, reign, and redeem creation.

The Historicity of Jesus

Many people doubt whether Jesus ever existed. But there are historians, even outside the Bible, who make mention of the Lord Jesus Christ.

1. Verified by Tacitus

   The Roman historian, Tacitus, writing around A.D. 114, tells us that the founder of the Christian religion, Jesus Christ, was put to death by Pontius Pilate in the reign of the Roman Emperor Tiberius (*Annals* 15.44).

2. Verified by Pliny the Younger

   Pliny the Younger wrote a letter to the Emperor Trajan on the subject of Christ and Christians (*Letters* 10.96-97).

3. Verified by Josephus

   Josephus, a Jewish historian writing in A.D. 90 (about the time John wrote Revelation), has a short biographical note on Jesus: "Now there was . . . Jesus, a wise man, if it be lawful to call Him a man, for He was a doer of wonderful works, a teacher of such men as received the truth with pleasure. He drew over to Him both many of the Jews and many of the Gentiles. He was Christ. And when Pilate at the suggestion of the principal men among us had condemned Him to the cross, those that loved Him at the first did not forsake Him for He appeared to them alive again the third day as the divine prophets had foretold these and ten thousand other wonderful things concerning Him. And the tribe of Christians so named from Him are not extinct at this day" (*Antiquities* 18.63).

4. Verified by the Talmud

   The Talmud refers to Jesus of Nazareth (*Sanhedrin* 43*a*, *Abodah Zerah* 16*b*-17*a*).

The apostle John said, "By this ye know the Spirit of God: every spirit that confesseth that Jesus Christ is come in the flesh is of God; and every spirit that confesseth not that Jesus Christ is come in the flesh is not of God; and this is that spirit of antichrist" (1 John 4:2-3). People who deny that God came in human flesh are of the antichrist. Jesus was a man of history.

D. His Resurrection

Jesus Christ had to be more than a man; He also had to be God. If Jesus were only a man, even the best of men, He could not have saved man from his sin. If He were even the right man from the seed of David, but not God, He could not have withstood the punishment of God the Father at the cross and risen from the dead. He could not have overcome Satan and the world but would have been conquered as all men are conquered.

1. The declaration of His sonship (v. 4a)

"Declared to be the Son of God with power, according to the spirit of holiness, by the resurrection from the dead."

If there was ever any question that Jesus was the Son of God, His resurrection from the dead should have ended it. He had to be man to reach us, but He had to be God to lift us up. He became a Son by His virgin birth and was affirmed a Son again at the resurrection. If someone said, "I am the Son of God," yet was a phony, God would not have raised him from the dead. The Lord would never play into the hands of a phony. Since God raised Christ from the dead, it affirmed that what He said was true.

a) The boundary

The key to understanding this verse is the word *declared*. It comes from the Greek word *horizō*, which means "boundary." We get our English word *horizon* from it. It refers to the clear demarcation line between the earth and sky. Paul is saying there may have been questions in the minds of some about whether Jesus was the Son of God, but because of the resurrection the line was drawn in absolute clarity: Jesus Christ *is* God in human flesh. As clearly as the horizon divides the earth from the sky, so the resurrection divides Jesus from the rest of humanity. When God raised Jesus Christ from the dead, He was irrefutably distinguished from all other human beings.

b) The beauty

The good news is that God became a man and then came into man's box. Not only can He get back out of the box because of His deity, but He can also take men with Him. In the early part of this century, the United States Congress issued a special edition of Thomas Jefferson's Bible. Jefferson had gone through and eliminated all references to the supernatural. All he wanted of Jesus in his Bible were some historical facts and moral teaching. The last statement in his gospel account reads, "There laid they Jesus: and rolled a great stone to the door of the sepulcher, and departed." That is where the life of Christ ended for Thomas Jefferson. But that is not where the gospel ends! Thank God the Bible ends with the fact that He is risen and is coming back for His children. I marvel at the majesty of the Lord Jesus Christ—the good news of God.

Focusing on the Facts

1. Man's eternal soul is made in such a way that it knows no _____ until it finds its _____ in God (see p. 25).
2. True or False: The issue isn't *whether* man will worship but only *what* he will worship (see p. 25).
3. Describe man's predicament inside his box (see p. 25).
4. What is man's only solution in escaping the box? What good news does Paul speak of Romans 1:1 (see p. 26)?
5. How can Paul say in any way that the gospel of Christ is his (see p. 27)?
6. True or False: That we don't deserve the good news makes it all the more true that God is gracious (see p. 28).

7. What were Jesus and Paul accused of? Show from Scripture how the gospel has continuity with the Old Testament (see pp. 30-31).
8. What does the phrase "by his prophets in the Holy Scriptures" refer to? What would the Jewish person have perceived from that statement (see p. 32)?
9. Describe the origin of Scripture (see pp. 32-33).
10. Explain the names and titles of the Son of God and describe their significance (see p. 34).
11. Discuss what the Sonship of Christ means. Explain how Jesus made the transition from His lofty position with God the Father to the position of dwelling with sinful man. Base your answer from Scripture (see pp. 34-36).
12. What's the difference in Christ being a Son eternally or becoming one at His incarnation (see p. 37)?
13. One of the reasons Jesus left His place in heaven was to experience _____ and become our _____ high priest (see p. 37).
14. What would have occurred at the cross if Jesus were only a man (see p. 39)?
15. As clearly as the horizon divides the earth from the sky, so the _____ divides Jesus from the rest of humanity (see pp. 39-40).

Pondering the Principles

1. Both Jesus and Paul were accused of denying the law of God and preaching a new message that contradicted the Old Testament. However they were simply contradicting the Jewish tradition that had obscured the Scripture. Look up the following passages and show how God has always promised the gospel of Christ: Luke 24:26-27, Acts 10:43, 26:6, Titus 1:2. Ask God to allow you to share this consistent message with someone else.

2. The central message of Christianity is Jesus Christ. From eternity He has been the second Person of the Trinity. He assumed the role of a Son in His incarnation. Jesus became a man to experience our humanness and to sympathize with us as our high priest. Not only did Jesus experience human birth and life but also death—on a cross. Do you believe Jesus Christ is who He says He is? Do you believe He had a miraculous virgin birth, sinless life, and died and rose for man's sin? If you have never

41

made a commitment to Christ, admit your sinfulness to Him and ask Him to forgive you of your sin.

3
The Provision, Proclamation, Privilege, and Purpose of the Good News

Outline

Introduction
A. The Illustration
B. The Inheritance

Review
 I. The Preacher of the Good News (v. 1)
 II. The Promise of the Good News (v. 2)
III. The Person of the Good News (vv. 3-4)
   A. His Name
   B. His Sonship
   C. His Birth
   D. His Resurrection
      1. The declaration of His sonship (v. 4*a*)

Lesson
      2. The demonstration of the Spirit (v. 4*b*)
         a) Matthew 3:16-17
         b) Matthew 12:31-32
         c) Luke 4:1
         d) John 3:34-35
IV. The Provision of the Good News (v. 5*a*)
   A. Grace from the King
      1. Unmerited favor
         a) Ephesians 2:8-9
         b) Romans 3:24
      2. Undeserved favor
         a) Romans 5:20-21
         b) Romans 3:20

Introduction

A. The Illustration

There's a story about an extremely wealthy man who possessed vast treasures of art. The man had only one son, who was an ordinary boy. The child died in his adolescence. The father greatly mourned his son's death. A few months after the death of his son, the father died as well.

The father stipulated in his will that all his possessions and art treasures were to be auctioned. He added that one particular painting was to be auctioned first. It was a painting of his son by an artist whom no one knew. The auctioneer, in accord with the man's wishes, directed the crowd to the painting of the obscure son. He started the bidding. Since no one knew the boy or the artist, the bidding was silent.

After a long time had passed, an old man who had been a servant in the house of the wealthy man said he would like to place a one-dollar bid on the portrait. He wanted to buy the painting because he had loved the son. A dollar was all he could afford to pay. There were no other bids, and the servant was able to purchase the painting. Then the auctioneer read the next portion of the will. It said: "All the rest of my treasure shall go to the one who loved my son enough to purchase his portrait."

B. The Inheritance

As that story suggests, there is no way to comprehend the riches God has provided for those who love His Son. The treasures prepared for those who love Him are infinite. Jesus said, "The kingdom of heaven is like a treasure hidden in a field, which when a man hath found, he hideth, and for joy of it goeth and selleth all that he hath, and buyeth that field" (Matt. 13:44). Paul said, "Eye hath not seen, nor ear heard, neither have entered into the heart of man, the things which God hath prepared for them that love him" (1 Cor. 2:9).

The good news is if we love the Son of God, we inherit all the riches of the Father. If we believe in Christ, we have treasure beyond imagination.

The message of the book of Romans is that God has good news for those who love His Son. The first seven verses of Romans contain the seed truth that blooms to its fullest in the remaining sixteen chapters.

I. THE PREACHER OF THE GOOD NEWS (v. 1; see pp. 13-21)

II. THE PROMISE OF THE GOOD NEWS (v. 2; see pp. 30-33)

III. THE PERSON OF THE GOOD NEWS (vv. 3-4; see pp. 33-40)

A. His Name (see p. 34)

The person of the good news is Christ Himself. It is what you do with God's Son—the Lord Jesus Christ—that determines whether you will inherit the riches of the Father. Jesus was a real human being, but He was also God. He had to be a man to take man's place on the cross, yet He also had to be God to conquer sin, death, hell, and Satan.

B. His Sonship (see pp. 34-36)

Jesus was made a Son at His incarnation. He was proved to be the Son of God at His resurrection. He has always existed as the Second Person of the Trinity, but there was also a time when Christ was made a Son and dwelt among men (cf. John 1:1, 14).

C. His Birth (see pp. 36-37)

D. His Resurrection (see pp. 39-40)

1. The declaration of His Sonship (v. 4a; see pp. 39-40)

Lesson

2. The demonstration of the Spirit (v. 4b)

"According to the spirit of holiness."

The Spirit of holiness is another way of referring to the Holy Spirit. Through the power of the Holy Spirit, Christ was able to accomplish His public ministry.

Christ expressed His power and was raised from the dead through the agency of the Holy Spirit.

a) Matthew 3:16-17—Matthew said, "When he [Jesus] was baptized, went up straightway out of the water; and, lo, the heavens were opened unto him, and he saw the Spirit of God descending like a dove, and lighting upon him. And, lo, a voice from heaven, saying, This is my beloved Son, in whom I am well pleased."

Within the Trinity there is equality, yet when Jesus took on human flesh, He submitted Himself as a Son to the will of the Father through the power of the Holy Spirit. Christ's baptism was the public confirmation of His ministry by God the Father and God the Holy Spirit. From that time on, Christ's ministry was controlled by the power of the Holy Spirit.

b) Matthew 12:31-32—Jesus said to the religious leaders, "All manner of sin and blasphemy shall be forgiven men; but the blasphemy against the Holy Spirit shall not be forgiven men. And whosoever speaketh a word against the Son of man, it shall be forgiven him; but whosoever speaketh against the Holy Spirit, it shall not be forgiven him." The Pharisees had been given enough physical evidence to believe in Christ, and yet they attributed His work to Satan. When they blasphemed His works, they were blaspheming the Spirit because it was the Spirit who was working through Him.

c) Luke 4:1—"Jesus, being full of the Holy Spirit, returned from the Jordan." After His baptism, Jesus was completely controlled and influenced by the Spirit of God.

d) John 3:34-35—When God the Father gave the Son the Spirit, He gave Him the Spirit in His absolute and utter fullness: "God giveth not the Spirit by measure unto him. The Father loveth the Son, and hath given all things into his hand."

47

The Son took on a role requiring voluntary submission and did only the will of the Father through the power of the Spirit. That is an amazing act of love and humility from One who is fully God and will be throughout eternity. It is important to recognize the Spirit's work in the ministry and resurrection of Jesus because it indicates that the entire Trinity was involved in the redemption of mankind. The greatest affirmation that Jesus is who He claimed to be is that the Father raised the Son through the agency of the Holy Spirit.

Marveling at the Humanity and Deity of Christ

The humanity and deity of Christ is a mysterious union we can never fully understand. But regardless of what we can or cannot understand, the Bible emphasizes both.

1. Matthew 17:24-27—Matthew said, "When they [the disciples] were come to Capernaum, they that received tribute money came to Peter, and said, Doth not your master pay tribute? He saith, Yes. And when he was come into the house, Jesus spoke first to him, saying, What thinkest thou, Simon? Of whom do the kings of the earth take custom or tribute? Of their own sons, or of strangers? Peter saith unto him, Of strangers. Jesus said unto him, Then are the sons free. Notwithstanding, lest we should offend them, go thou to the sea, and cast an hook, and take up the fish that first cometh up. And when thou hast opened its mouth, thou shalt find a piece of money; that take, and give unto them for me and thee." By paying His taxes, Jesus was showing His humanness. But directing Peter to go down to the sea and taking money from a fish's mouth was a display of His deity. He paid His taxes, but He had ways of providing those taxes that were absolutely supernatural.

2. Mark 4:35-39—Jesus said to His disciples, "The same day, when the evening was come, he saith unto them, Let us pass over unto the other side. And when they had sent away the multitude, they took him even as he was in the boat. And there were also with him other little boats. And there arose a great storm of wind, and the waves beat into the boat, so that it was now full. And he was in the stern of the boat, asleep on a pillow; and they awake him, and say unto him, Master, carest thou not that we perish? And he arose, and rebuked the wind, and said unto the

sea, Peace, be still. And the wind ceased, and there was a great calm." In His humanness, Jesus was tired and asleep in the storm. But in His deity, He caused the elements to obey His voice.

3. Luke 23:39-43—At the cross "one of the malefactors who were hanged railed at him, saying, If thou be the Christ, save thyself and us. But the other, answering, rebuked him, saying, Dost not thou fear God, seeing thou art in the same condemnation? And we, indeed, justly; for we receive the due reward of our deeds. But this man hath done nothing amiss. And he said unto Jesus, Lord, remember me when thou comest into thy kingdom. And Jesus said unto him, Verily I say unto thee, Today shalt thou be with me in paradise." In His humanness, Jesus was a victim, mercilessly hammered to a cross after being spat upon, mocked, and humiliated. But in His deity, He promised the thief on the cross eternal life as only God can.

IV. THE PROVISION OF THE GOOD NEWS (v. 5a)

"By whom we have received grace and apostleship."

A. Grace from the King

Every believer receives the grace of God by responding to the good news. Paul could be saying he had received the grace of apostleship. But I think he was saying much more than that. The good news is that salvation is by grace.

1. Unmerited favor

a) Ephesians 2:8-9—Paul said, "For by grace are ye saved through faith; and that not of yourselves, it is the gift of God—not of works, lest any man should boast." The grace of God that brings salvation has appeared to all men. It is totally apart from anything man could ever do to receive God's favor. It is the unmerited favor of God, who in His mercy and loving-kindness grants us salvation as a gift. All we do is simply respond by believing in His Son.

b) Romans 3:24—Paul also said we are "justified freely by his grace through the redemption that is in Christ Jesus." Paul then says in verse 27, "Where is boasting then? It is excluded. By what law? Of works? Nay, but by the law of faith." We enter the kingdom of God only by the grace of God. There is no place for self-congratulations or human achievement in the kingdom of God. We are not saved by any innate sense of our good deeds or works.

2. Undeserved favor

Salvation does not come by confirmation, communion, baptism, church membership, church attendance, trying to keep the Ten Commandments, or living out the Sermon on the Mount. It does not come by giving to charity or even believing that there is a God. It does not come by simply being moral and respectable. Salvation does not even come by claiming to be a Christian. Salvation comes only when we receive by faith the gift of God's grace. Hell will be full of people who have tried to get to heaven in other ways.

a) Romans 5:20-21—Paul said, "The law entered, that the offense might abound. But where sin abounded, grace did much more abound; that as sin hath reigned unto death, even so might grace reign through righteousness unto eternal life by Jesus Christ, our Lord." The first provision of the gospel is grace that is neither earned nor deserved. You couldn't earn it even if you wanted to.

b) Romans 3:20—Paul also said, "By the deeds of the law there shall no flesh be justified in his sight."

Donald Grey Barnhouse said, "Love that gives upward is worship; love that goes outward is affection; love that stoops is grace" (*Expositions of Bible Doctrines Taking the Epistle to the Romans as a Point of Departure*, vol. 1 [Grand Rapids: Eerdmans, 1952], p. 72). God has stooped to give man grace, even though we don't deserve it. The dying saint Pauson said, "Grace is the only thing that can make us like God. I might be dragged through heaven, earth, and hell and I would still be the same sinful, polluted, wretch unless God Himself should cleanse me by His grace." Grace is a free gift to man from God.

B. **Service to the King**

Verse 5 says, "By whom we have received grace and apostleship." Many might say Paul is referring only to the apostles, but I believe he is embracing the entire believing community in this passage. We have received a different kind of apostleship.

1. The broad sense of the title

The gospel not only brings us the grace of salvation, but the task of apostleship—being sent to preach the good news to others.

a) Hebrews 3:1—The writer of Hebrews said, "Holy brethren, partakers of the heavenly calling, consider the Apostle and High Priest of our profession, Christ Jesus." The term *apostle* must be seen in this wider sense because Christ Himself is called one. He was sent from the Father. In its broadest sense, the term refers to any gospel messenger. Commentator William Hendriksen wrote that an apostle is "anyone who is sent on a spiritual mission, anyone who in that capacity represents His Sender and brings the message of salvation" (*Exposition of Paul's Epistle to the Romans* [Grand Rapids: Baker, 1981], p. 38). We are called and saved to be sent to reach the world.

b) Romans 16:7—Paul said, "Greet Andronicus and Junias, my kinsmen and my fellow prisoners, who are of note among the apostles, who also were in Christ before me." What kind of apostles were Andronicus and Junias? They were certainly not official apostles with a capital "A" but were sent to proclaim the truth of Christ in His behalf. Paul is saying there is not only the grace of salvation but the challenge of being sent.

c) Acts 14:14—Both Barnabas and Paul are here referred to as apostles. Barnabas wasn't one of the twelve apostles, nor was he the equivalent of Paul, but he was one who was sent. The term *apostle* is broadened in many biblical texts so it can't be confined to the twelve.

2. The unique sense of the term

There is no question that Paul's apostleship was unique. There was no other apostle like him. He had a special call from God to be the apostle to the Gentiles, yet he was an apostle as truly as any of the others who saw Christ personally after the resurrection. It is true that all believers are "sent ones"—a literal definition of the word *apostles*—but not all believers are apostles in the first-century sense. Nevertheless, each believer is called to reach the world for Christ.

No Spectators in the Christian Life

I grew up with an athletic background. I played on many different teams in various sports programs through the years. I can remember several times when a youth with little or no athletic ability would try out for a team. Every once in a while a coach would feel sorry for such a boy and place him on the team in spite of his performance. Maybe his father had died or he was poor—the kind of youth that drew sympathy. He would be given a uniform and made to feel a part of the team but would never be given a chance to play.

That analogy points to the opposite case in our Christian life. The Lord doesn't place you on the team just so you can sit on the bench. He intends to send you into the game. It is His grace that calls you to salvation, but He will also send you as an apostle into the world to witness for Him. We are all like the youth who has no ability. God graciously puts us on the team, not because of our own ability, but purely by His sovereign grace. And He gives us the ability to play the game. We have the holy privilege of serving Jesus Christ.

3. The compelling sense of the task

Do you have any comprehension of what a high calling it is to serve Christ?

a) Ephesians 2:10—Paul said, "We are his workmanship, created in Christ Jesus unto good works, which God hath before ordained that we should walk in them."

b) Ephesians 4:1—Paul said, "I therefore, the prisoner of the Lord, beseech you that ye walk worthy of the vocation to which ye are called."

It is said a victor at the Olympic Games in ancient times was asked, "Spartan, what will you gain by this victory?" He replied, "I, sir, shall have the honor to fight on the front line for my king." We're called to serve even with all our limitations.

A High and Holy Calling

1. Illustrated by D. L. Moody

At the close of an address by D. L. Moody, a highly educated man said to him coldly, "Excuse me, but you made eleven mistakes in your grammar tonight." Mr. Moody replied, "I probably did. My early education was very faulty. But I am using all the grammar that I know in the Master's service. How about you?" (Cited in A. Naismith's *1200 Notes, Quotes and Anecdotes* [Chicago: Moody, 1962], p. 179.)

On another occasion a man came up to Moody and said, "I don't like your invitation. I don't think it's the right way to do it." Moody said, "I appreciate that. I've always been uncomfortable with it, too. I wish I knew a better way. What is your method of inviting people to Christ?" "Oh," the man said, "I don't have one." Moody replied, "Then I like mine better." Whatever our limitations, God has sent us to reach the world.

2. Illustrated by Donald Grey Barnhouse

Donald Barnhouse, a well known commentator, reflected on an interesting time in his life when he was being ordained into the Presbyterian ministry:

"The moderator of the Presbytery asked me questions, and I answered them. They told me to kneel down. Men came toward me, and one man was asked to make the prayer. I felt his hand come on my head, and then the hands of others touching my head, and pressing down on his and the other hands. The ring of men closed in, and one man began to pray. It was a nice little prayer and had one pat little phrase in it, 'Father, guard him with Thy love, guide him with Thine eye and gird him with Thy power.'

"I kept thinking about those three verbs, guard, guide and gird. It seemed as foolish as performing a marriage ceremony upon two people who had been living together for a quarter of a century and who had a family of children together. I knew I had been ordained long since, and that the Hands that had been on my head were Hands that had been pierced, and nailed to a cross.

"Years later the man that made the prayer that day signed a paper saying that he was opposed to the doctrine of the virgin birth, the doctrine of the deity of Jesus Christ, the doctrine of the substitutionary atonement, the doctrine of the miracles of Christ, the doctrine of the inspiration of the Scriptures, as tests for ordination or a man's good standing in the ministry.

"When I read his name on that list, I put my hand on the top of my head and smiled to myself wondering how many dozen times I had had my hair cut since his unholy hands had touched me. And I had the profound consolation of knowing that the hand of the Lord Jesus Christ, wounded and torn because of my sins, had touched me and given me an apostleship which was from God and which was more important than any that men could approve by their little ceremonies" (*Expositions of Bible Doctrines Taking the Epistle to the Romans as a Point of Departure* [Grand Rapids: Eerdmans, 1952], pp. 76-77: used by permission).

Donald Barnhouse's experience caused me to think of my own ordination. Good and godly men were there who asked me all kinds of questions. They came up and they put their hands on me and prayed. They also signed my ordination certificate. There weren't enough lines for them to write their names so they started writing their names all over the paper. There was one name written bigger than any other name, and it appears on the first line of my certificate.

Not long after, the man who wrote on the first line of my certificate abandoned the ministry, involved himself in replete immorality, denied his faith in Christ, became an outspoken atheist, and finally a philosophy professor at the University of Southern California.

I, like Dr. Barnhouse, thank God that my apostleship—my ministry—didn't come from men but from Christ Himself.

V. THE PROCLAMATION OF THE GOOD NEWS (vv. 5b, 6)

"For obedience to the faith among all nations . . . among whom are ye also the called of Jesus Christ."

Paul is saying that just as you have been called to Christ, you will go out and call others to Christ. The good news concerning Jesus Christ leads us to proclaim the same good news to all the nations of the earth.

A. Man Designed for Obedience to Christ (v. 5b)

"Obedience to the faith."

Paul says the same thing in Romans 16:26: "According to the commandment of the everlasting God, made known to all nations for the obedience of faith." The result of faith is obedience. Show me someone who says he believes in Christ and lives a life of disobedience, and I'll show you someone who is not redeemed.

1. Dead faith

Faith, if it does not manifest itself in works of obedience, is dead. James said, "Wilt thou know, O vain man, that faith without works is dead?" (James 2:20). We are not saved *by* works, but we are saved *unto* good

55

works. Christianity is a call for people to be obedient to the faith. When you put your faith in Christ, you affirm your obedience to Him.

Paul used a definite article in describing this faith, similar to Jude, who spoke of "*the* faith which was once delivered unto the saints" (Jude 3, emphasis added). It refers to the actual content of the gospel message—the process of "teaching them to observe all things whatsoever I have commanded you" (Matt. 28:20). Sadly, that isn't the message many people are hearing today. We must call people to faith, but to a faith that obeys the Word of God. People who say they believe and then live a life of disobedience do not possess genuine saving faith. People who believe in Christ will obey Him.

2. Obedient faith

It is not that faith plus obedience equals salvation, but that obedient faith equals salvation. True faith is verified in one's obedience to God. Because Jesus is Lord, He demands obedience. There is no faith without obedience. Paul said to the Roman Christians, "I thank my God through Jesus Christ for you all, that your faith is spoken of throughout the whole world" (1:8). And why is it their faith was spoken of throughout the world? Romans 16:19 says, "Your obedience is come abroad unto all men." In the beginning it is your faith that is spread abroad, but in the end it is your obedience. Why? Because one cannot exist without the other.

Liquor Store Christianity?

I was riding in an automobile with a man who was a professor at a theological seminary as we drove by a liquor store. I mentioned that it was an unusual-looking place. The man I was riding with said, "Yes, there is a chain of those stores all over the city, and they're all owned by one man." He went on to say that the man came to his Sunday school class. I said, "He does?" He said, "Yes, he's there every Sunday." He went on to say he was in his discipleship group and that they meet every week. I said, "Does it bother him that he owns all those liquor stores?" The professor replied, "We've certainly talked a lot about it. He feels people are going to buy liquor anyway, so why not buy it from him." I asked, "Is the rest of his life in order?" The professor responded, "He did leave his wife and is living with a young girl." The professor then said, "You know, sometimes it is so hard for me to understand how a Christian can live like that." I said, "Have you ever thought about the possibility that he may not be a Christian at all?"

A Christian recognizes the lordship of Christ. Romans 10:9-10 says, "If thou shalt confess with thy mouth the Lord Jesus, and shalt believe in thine heart that God hath raised him from the dead, thou shalt be saved. For with the heart man believeth unto righteousness; and with the mouth confession is made unto salvation." Faith that excludes obedience won't save anyone. The delusion that it will causes many people to take the broad road that leads to destruction (Matt. 7:13-14). That's like building a religious super-structure on sand (Matt. 7:21-29).

B. Man Designated for Evangelism on Behalf of Christ (v. 6)

"Among whom are ye also the called of Jesus Christ."

Believers have been called to faith in Christ. We have come out of a life of disobedience into a life of obedience, from unbelief into faith. And because we have been called ourselves, we are obliged to call others to faith in Christ.

VI. THE PRIVILEGES OF THE GOOD NEWS (v. 7)

"To all that be in Rome, beloved of God, called to be saints: grace to you and peace from God our Father, and the Lord Jesus Christ."

That verse mentions three privileges believers have as a result of the good news.

A. Beloved of God (v. 7*a*)

"To all that be in Rome, beloved of God."

1. Ephesians 2:4-5—"God, who is rich in mercy, for his great love with which he loved us, even when we were dead in sins, hath made us alive together with Christ." God loved us even when we were dead in sin.

2. 1 John 3:1—The apostle John said, "Behold, what manner of love the Father hath bestowed upon us, that we should be called the children of God." The phrase translated "what manner" comes from the Greek word *potapān*, which means, "something foreign." It has to do with something that is other-worldly. God's love for mankind is so different from any other kind of love, it's as if it's from another planet!

3. Ephesians 1:6—We have been accepted in the Beloved One "to the praise of the glory of his grace." God loves us in His Son.

4. Romans 5:5—"The love of God is shed abroad in our hearts by the Holy Spirit who is given unto us."

5. Romans 8:35—Paul asked rhetorically, "What shall separate us from the love of Christ?" The answer, of course, is nothing. Those who act on the good news are beloved of God, which is to receive His infinite blessing.

B. Called of God (v. 7*b*)

"Called to be saints."

This is the effectual call to salvation. We are saved by the sovereign act of God.

1. The general call

There are passages in the Bible that speak of a general call to be saved.

a) Isaiah 45:22—The Lord said, "Be saved, all the ends of the earth; for I am God, and there is none else."

b) Isaiah 55:6—Isaiah declared, "Seek ye the Lord while he may be found, call ye upon him while he is near."

c) Ezekiel 33:11—Ezekiel said, "Turn ye, turn from your evil ways."

d) Matthew 11:28—Jesus said, "Come unto me, all ye that labor and are heavy laden, and I will give you rest."

e) John 7:37—Jesus also said, "If any man thirst, let him come unto me, and drink."

f) Revelation 22:17—"The Spirit and the bride say, Come. And let him that heareth say, Come. And let him that is athirst come. And whosoever will, let him take the water of life freely."

g) Romans 10:17—Paul said, "Faith cometh by hearing, and hearing by the word of God."

2. The specific call

Paul is not simply giving a general call to receive the gospel in verse 7. He has in mind the effectual call to redemption that comes by the sovereign will of God. The word *called* is another word for "the elect." Ephesians 1:4 says, "He hath chosen us in him before the foundation of the world." Scripture is filled with references to anyone who believes as one who has been sovereignly called and predestinated by God. From man's viewpoint, we come to Christ as an act of our will. But from God's perspective, He called us to Himself before the world began.

C. Saints of God (v. 7c)

"To all that be in Rome, beloved of God, called to be saints."

There should be a comma after the word *called* because the words *to be* do not appear in the Greek text. If you are a Christian, you are a saint. The Greek word for "saint" is *hagios*, which means "holy one." By virtue of being beloved of God and called to salvation, believers have been set apart from the world in obedience to God.

1. The meaning of "set apart" in the Old Testament

In the Old Testament, many things were said to be set apart. The Holy of Holies was set apart (Ex. 26:33) along with the tithe (Lev. 27:30) and the priests (Lev. 21:6-7). Exodus 19:6 says the whole nation of Israel was set apart. That was simply a way of saying that all those things were holy—set apart unto God.

2. The meaning of "set apart" in the New Testament

The New Testament does not describe those Old Testament concepts as holy anymore. The Holy of Holies doesn't exist because the veil was torn when Christ died (Matt. 27:51). The Temple has been destroyed. The tithe does not apply anymore because Christians are not under a theocracy. The priests aren't needed anymore because of the priesthood of believers (1 Pet. 2:9). The nation of Israel has been temporarily set aside (Rom. 9). Christians are holy—set apart—because the new temple of God is the church. We're set apart from our sins unto God (Heb. 2:11; Acts 26:18).

D. Blessed by God (v. 7d)

"Grace to you and peace from God our Father, and the Lord Jesus Christ."

The only people who could ever receive such a benediction would be those who were beloved, called, and made holy by God. Believers are the only ones who could receive His grace and experience His peace.

VII. THE PURPOSE OF THE GOOD NEWS (v. 5c)

"For his name."

A. The Primary Purpose—God's Glory

The phrase "for his name" simply means that the purpose of the good news is that everything should focus on the glory of God. Many people think the main reason God saves people is so He can keep them out of hell, or so they can experience His love, or lead their lives. But all those reasons are secondary.

People are to be saved for the glory of God because it is an affront to His holy name that someone should live in rebellion against Him. That people experience salvation is not the main issue with God. It is His glory that is at stake.

1. 3 John 7—John said of faithful believers, "For his name's sake they went forth, taking nothing of the Gentiles."

2. Philippians 2:9-11—Paul said of Jesus, "God . . . hath highly exalted him, and given him a name which is above every name, that at the name of Jesus every knee should bow, of things in heaven, and things in earth, and things under the earth, and that every tongue should confess that Jesus Christ is Lord, to the glory of God, the Father." Salvation is for God's glory.

3. 2 Corinthians 4:15—Paul wished that "the abundant grace might through the thanksgiving of many redound to the glory of God."

B. The Secondary Purpose—Man's Salvation

God is glorified when someone believes His gospel. He is glorified when men love His Son. He is glorified when men accept His diagnosis of their greatest need, which is forgiveness of sin. Although man benefits from God's provision of salvation, a Christian exists for the glory of God.

Madame Guyon, the seventeenth century French mystic, wrote this in her poem "Glory to God Alone" (vol. II, *Cantique* 15):

61

Glorious, Almighty, First, and without end!
When wilt Thou melt the mountains, and descend!
When wilt Thou shoot abroad Thy conqu'ring rays
And teach these atoms Thou hast made Thy praise?

The good news comes from God. It was promised in the Old Testament and it is personified in the Lord Jesus Christ. It provides grace and service, is proclaimed by those who receive eternal privileges, and is ultimately for the purpose of glorifying God.

Focusing on the Facts

1. What does Scripture say about the riches of God for those who love Him (see p. 45)?
2. What is the message of the book of Romans (see p. 45)?
3. True or False: The Spirit of holiness is another way of saying the Holy Spirit (see p. 46).
4. What does it mean to blaspheme the Holy Spirit (Matt. 12:31-32; see p. 47)?
5. Explain the voluntary submission of Christ as the Son of God (see pp. 47-48).
6. What are two provisions of the good news? Explain both, using biblical examples (see pp. 49-51).
7. What is the high and holy calling of the Christian (see pp. 52-53)?
8. The Christian has been designed for two things. What are they (see pp. 55-57)?
9. The result of faith is _____ (see p. 55).
10. True or False: Christianity is a call for people to be obedient to the faith (see p. 56).
11. What are the privileges of the good news? Explain from the Scripture how God loves man (see pp. 57-58).
12. Differentiate between God's general call and God's special call to salvation (see pp. 58-59).
13. Explain what it means to be a saint of God (see p. 60).
14. What is the primary purpose for proclaiming the good news of God (see p. 61)?
15. What is the secondary purpose for proclaiming the good news (see p. 61)?

Pondering the Principles

1. There are many things a person receives as a result of becoming a Christian, but one of the most notable is the grace of God. Ephesians 2:8-9 says, "For by grace are ye saved through faith; and that not of yourselves, it is the gift of God—not of works, lest any man should boast." If you are not a Christian, read the following passages and ask God to show you His grace—His unmerited favor—that is available to you: Acts 15:11, Romans 3:23-26, and Romans 11:5-6.

2. When a person becomes a Christian, not only does he receive the grace of God, but he is also called to witness about His grace. The Christian is to live a life of obedience and to call others into that same life of faith. Do you witness to others about your faith? Is it clear to those around you that Christ is the most important thing to you? If you are not presently witnessing by what you say and what you do, ask God to make evangelism a consistent part of your life.

3. The primary purpose of the good news is the glory of God. It is an affront to God that someone should live in rebellion against Him. Study the following passages and determine in your heart that you will properly represent the name of God on earth: Malachi 1:11-14, Acts 15:14, and Colossians 3:1-17.

4
Marks of True Spiritual Service—Part 1

Outline

Introduction
A. Wrong Motives for Serving the Lord
    1. Panic
    2. Prestige
    3. Pride
    4. Peer pressure
    5. Parents
    6. Profit
B. Right Motives for Serving the Lord
    1. The fight for right motives
    2. The fervency for right motives
        a) Paul was an initiator
        b) Paul was an intellectual
        c) Paul was intimate
    3. The focus on right motives
        a) Paul's knowledge of externalism
        b) Paul's knack for internalism
            (1) Paul's spirit
            (2) Paul's service
                (*a*) Romans 12:1-2
                (*b*) Philippians 3:3
                (*c*) Acts 27:22-23
                (*d*) 2 Timothy 1:3
                (*e*) 2 Timothy 2:22

Lesson

Introduction

A. Wrong Motives for Serving the Lord

   1. Panic

      Some people serve the Lord because of legalism. They try to keep lists of dos and don'ts because they are afraid not to. They think that is what God requires if you're to get into the kingdom. Some cults teach that if you don't

66

go to the mission field for at least two years, you won't make it into heaven. Within the framework of Christianity, some people serve the Lord strictly because they feel bound to do so. They want to keep God from breaking their bubble and making life miserable for them.

2. Prestige

Others want to make a name for themselves and be highly esteemed by others. They seek the chief seats, playing the role of Diotrephes, who loved "to have the pre-eminence" (3 John 9).

3. Pride

There are some people who serve the Lord because they want to be thought of as religious. For them, Christianity is a way to feed their egos.

4. Peer pressure

There are some people who serve the Lord because of peer pressure. Since everyone else is doing it, they've got to get on the bandwagon. They think that if they're not involved, they won't be accepted by their group.

5. Parents

There are also some people who serve the Lord because they have been forced to by their parents. They might have been intimidated for years and still feel bound by that kind of intimidation.

6. Profit

Some people serve the Lord for money. They are simply out for the almighty dollar. Jesus, for them, is a commodity that sells.

Any of the above reasons for service, however, betray external motives. They are motivated not by a pure response from the heart but by an unrighteous response from the flesh.

B. Right Motives for Serving the Lord

1. The fight for right motives

All who serve the Lord struggle from time to time with having the purest of motives. You can easily find yourself drawn into service with a wrong motive. There are times when I preach, not because I want to, but because I have to. It can become a mechanical function.

Example 1

There are times when someone teaches a Bible class because they think that in doing so, they will be looked upon as spiritual and gain a position of leadership. There are times when a group will ask me to come and speak to them and my first thought is, *The last time I spoke there, they only gave me twenty-five dollars.* But that is the devil simply trying to tempt me to preach with a wrong motive.

Example 2

I was once invited to speak at a university campus gathering on the credibility of Christianity, with each session followed by a forty-five minute question-and-answer period. I spoke for three consecutive Tuesday nights, driving fifty miles one way each time. I ultimately received three dollars for the entire event. They must have felt I was worth one dollar per night! I had just graduated from seminary, and money was scarce, so I had to carefully examine my motives. We can be easily tempted to think about the money instead of the ministry. We all find ourselves fighting improper motives as we serve Christ.

2. The fervency for right motives

In Romans 1:8-16*a*, the apostle Paul epitomizes what it really means to have the right perspective on true spiritual service. Although some 1900 years have passed since this passage was written, it is still relevant and alive with Paul's affection. As you study the passage, you can see Paul's great love for the church in Rome, a group he had never met. And it was not like him to build on another man's foundation (cf. Rom. 15:20).

a) Paul was an initiator

The apostle Paul is most often seen as a strong, determined, confrontive, bold, and dynamic individual.

b) Paul was an intellectual

Paul's logic was brilliant. He was a genius—the greatest theologian the church has ever known.

c) Paul was intimate

Paul was a sensitive, loving, warm, and gentle man of God. He had the zeal of a prophet, the mind of a teacher, the determination of an apostle, but also the heart of a shepherd. Paul was no paid preacher with the hope of a fee in place of his heart. He wasn't a preacher with a bag of old-hat sermons in place of passion. He had a true shepherd's heart.

disscussion what is your motive for serving Christ?

3. The focus on right motives

Before Paul moved into the full explanation of the good news, which begins in verse 16 and runs throughout the rest of the book, he wanted to open his heart to the believers in Rome. It was important for him to do so because the Christians in Rome didn't know him. They might have wondered why he was writing to them and why, if he was the great apostle to the Gentiles, he never came to their city before. Paul addressed those issues right at the beginning of his epistle to the Romans.

Because of his heart for people, Paul cared deeply about their spiritual maturity yet had been unable to come because God had not allowed him to. Since the Romans had never met him, the only way they could have had insight into his heart was if he wrote and then came to them. In Romans 1:8-16, the apostle opens his heart to reveal the character of his service for Christ.

discussion Is there some things you have wanted to do but God has not allowed it?

a) Paul's knowledge of externalism

Paul had been raised in Judaism and knew that the Romans might not be able to differentiate between real service to Christ and ritualism. He knew the external, religious activity of the Pharisees, Sadducees, scribes, chief priests, and elders. He knew that much of their service was merely routine and liturgy—physical, superficial, and temporal. Paul also grew up in a Gentile world and knew how the priests served their pagan gods They served out of the fear that if they didn't perform certain functions, the gods would crush them or bring calamity on their cities and towns. As a result, their service to the gods was shallow and superficial.

Look at Acts 9 — Saul/Paul's Conversation

b) Paul's knack for internalism

Paul summed up his entire perspective for the Romans in the statement "God . . . whom I serve with my spirit" (v. 9). He was saying that his service came from within, not from without. He served with a pure and holy motivation. What motivated him was not what people thought or what they paid. It wasn't peer pressure or some legal obligation but a heart motivated to accomplish the will of God.

(1) Paul's spirit

Paul affirmed that his whole heart, mind, soul, and spirit were involved in the service he rendered. For the apostle Paul, ministry was an all-out effort. He was sincere.

(2) Paul's service

We use the word *spirit* in the same way Paul used it. We may watch an athlete go all out in his performance, and comment, "That is spirited play!" That means he had his whole being involved in *Some colleges* his effort. ~~When I was in college~~, the "Esprit de Corps award" was given to the football player who rendered the most effort on the field. That is

70

the sense in which the apostle Paul served the Lord.

Paul never served the Lord without a wholehearted commitment. By doing that, he distinguished himself from the hirelings—those whose labor was external and insincere (John 10:11-13). He also separated himself from the heathen, cultic priests. Verse 9 tells us that the Holy Spirit was behind the scenes, energizing the service of the apostle Paul.

It is interesting to observe that the phrase translated "to serve" comes from the Greek verb *latreuō* and is frequently translated "worship." It is always used in the New Testament to refer to religious service or worship. Many think of worship as stained-glass windows and pipe organs. But the Bible says the same word that means worship also means service. The greatest worship you ever render to God is to serve Him. For Paul, service was a total commitment.

(*a*) Romans 12:1-2—After finishing his main theological treatises, Paul said, "I beseech you therefore, brethren, by the mercies of God, that ye present your bodies a living sacrifice, holy, acceptable unto God, which is your reasonable service. And be not conformed to this world, but be ye transformed by the renewing of your mind, that ye may prove what is that good, and acceptable, and perfect, will of God." With everything Paul had, he served to his fullest.

(*b*) Philippians 3:3—"We are the circumcision, who worship God in the spirit, and rejoice in Christ Jesus, and have no confidence in the flesh." Here Paul makes the same distinction between internal, spiritual worship, and external, fleshly worship.

(c) Acts 27:22-23—Paul, in the midst of a storm on the Mediterranean Sea, said, "I exhort you to be of good cheer; for there shall be no loss of any man's life among you, but only of the ship. For there stood by me this night an angel of God, whose I am, and whom I serve."

(d) 2 Timothy 1:3—Paul wrote, "I thank God, whom I serve from my forefathers with pure conscience." He was saying, "You can look deep inside me and see that I serve God with a whole heart." Paul's service was an act of worship. It was deep, genuine, and honest. That is the real measure of true spirituality. The only way to serve God is with total commitment.

(e) 2 Timothy 2:22—Paul said this to Timothy, who was wavering in his faith: "Flee also youthful lusts, but follow righteousness, faith, love, peace, with them that call on the Lord out of a pure heart."

Lesson

I. A THANKFUL SPIRIT (v. 8)

"First, I thank my God through Jesus Christ for you all, that your faith is spoken of throughout the whole world."

A. Paul's Pattern

If there's one thing we know about the apostle Paul, it's that he had a thankful heart. In almost every one of his epistles, Paul expressed thanks for the ones to whom he wrote. The only exception is the epistle to the Galatians. The Galatians had defected from the gospel and were functioning in the flesh. All the churches Paul wrote needed to be corrected, but even though he saw the need for instruction, he also could find something in them to be thankful for. He was always able to see God's purposes being accomplished. Paul expressed what is in the heart of all true servants of God—an attitude of gratitude.

Some people go through life dwelling on the negative. English novelist and poet Thomas Hardy said he had a friend who would be the first to spot the manure pile in a beautiful meadow! Some people refuse to be grateful for the good that God is doing in someone else's life. If it isn't happening to them, they think it's bad. The apostle Paul didn't express his thanks by saying, "I'm so thankful for what God has done for *me*"; rather he said, "I thank God for *you*." He received as much joy from someone else's success as he did from his own.

B. Paul's Predicament

Paul was in Corinth when he wrote this epistle. At the time, the Jewish leaders were plotting to kill him (Acts 20:3). But he never lost his perspective. Even in that particular situation he was filled with thanksgiving. When Paul was on his way to Jerusalem, he was constantly told he would be put in chains and his life would be in imminent danger. But it never bothered Paul in the least because he had a thankful heart.

C. Paul's Praise

What was Paul thankful about in Romans 1:8? That God had given the Romans a testimony of faith that was extending throughout the whole world. History records that the testimony of the church in Rome was so strong, Emperor Claudius expelled all the Jews in A.D. 49 (cf. Acts 18:2). The Roman historian Suetonius tells us why: "Since the Jews constantly made disturbances at the instigation of Chrestus, he expelled them from Rome" (*Life of Claudius* 25.4). "Chrestus" is the Latin spelling for Christ. The Roman Christians had such a tremendous testimony, they stirred up the entire Jewish community. The "whole world" of verse 8 has reference not to the whole world comprehensively, but the whole world of their understanding—the Mediterranean regions.

Superficial servers, unlike Paul, are never satisfied with their situations and are therefore thankless. They focus on their own insatiable appetites for glory. Show me a thankless heart, and I'll show you a proud, self-centered individual. Even when you can't find things in your own life to be thankful for, you can always find things that God is doing in someone else's life. You should be just as thankful for them as you would be for yourself. Philippians 2:3 says, "With humility of mind let each of you regard one another as more important than himself" (NASB*). The apostle Paul was thankful in the midst of his distresses because his joy came not from his own success, but from the advance of God's kingdom.

D. Paul's Passion

The intimacy Paul had with God was not something the other religions of his day could relate to. The pagans thought their gods were distant and so did the Jewish people. To Paul, God was not a theological abstraction but an intimate friend.

1. The source (v. 8a)

"First, I thank my God."

a) Philippians 1:3—"I thank my God upon every remembrance of you."

b) Philemon 4—"I thank my God, making mention of thee always in my prayers." Paul was so in tune with God's purposes that they became the source of his thanksgiving.

Paul said, "The Holy Spirit witnesseth in every city, saying that bonds and afflictions await me" (Acts 20:23). Even when he became a prisoner in the Mamertine prison, he maintained a thankful spirit. The Mamertine prison was connected to the city's sewage system, which ran by the prison door. The prisoners were either strangled or starved to death. Afterwards the guards

New American Standard Bible.

flooded the chamber to wash away the corpses of the victims.

Regardless of his condition, Paul remained thankful to God. He was consistently filled with joy because his joy had nothing to do with his present circumstances. He was concerned only about proclaiming the cause of Christ (cf. 1 Cor. 2:2).

2. The mediator (v. 8b)

"I thank my God through Jesus Christ."

Jesus is always seen as the Mediator between God and man (cf. 1 Tim. 2:5). The only way Paul could come to God was through Jesus Christ.

a) John 14:6—Jesus said, "No man cometh unto the Father, but by me."

b) Hebrews 4:16—The writer of Hebrews, having just spoken of Christ's mediatory role, said, "Let us, therefore, come boldly unto the throne of grace, that we may obtain mercy, and find grace to help in time of need." Apart from Jesus Christ, God would be to us nothing but a consuming fire (Heb. 12:29). The only reason we can approach God is that Christ died in our behalf. Paul served his God through Christ with a heart of thanksgiving.

3. The scope (v. 8c)

"I thank my God through Jesus Christ for you all."

The scope of Paul's thanksgiving was all-encompassing. By this statement, Paul showed that his heart was toward all the Roman believers. He was not biased nor did he choose favorites. He didn't look for what was wrong with people. He was simply thankful.

Many people are not thankful because they don't think they have what they deserve. But if you really received what you deserved, you would be in hell forever. Paul was thankful that the faith of the believers in Rome had been spoken of throughout the world. In saying he was thankful for their faith, he was referring to the genuineness of their salvation, and the clear testimony of their lives. He was thankful that they were a redeemed fellowship manifesting the life and the power of the Lord Jesus Christ, even in the midst of severe Roman persecution. Their faith added credibility and integrity to the message of Christianity.

Are You Truly Thankful?

Wouldn't it be honoring to God to be famous throughout the entire world for your faith? Some churches are famous for their pastor; others for their architecture. Some are famous for their art, others for their organ. Some are even famous for their choirs, or the different celebrities that attend. But wouldn't it be great to be famous around the world for your faith? People come to me almost daily and ask, "Could you recommend a good church in my city?" They don't say, "Could you recommend one with nice architecture or one with a pipe organ?" They want to attend a church where the pastor and the congregation believe God and take Him at His Word.

A thankful heart is essential for true spiritual service. If you are trying to serve the Lord without gratitude in your heart for what He's done for you, you are serving in the flesh with improper motives. One who is thankful realizes that God has a cause for everything that happens. One who serves externally, legalistically, or ritualistically will not find many things to be thankful for in his life because he is not grateful for the things God has already done for him.

Do you have a thankful heart? Are you overwhelmed with thanksgiving for what God has done? If you are, that will take out any bitterness or resentment you may be feeling toward God or anyone else. There is so much to be thankful for. The devil often tempts us by saying, "You deserve better than that. You don't have to be thankful." He attempts to play a game with our minds, but when he does, step back and say, "No! There is too much to be thankful for!"

II. A CONCERNED SPIRIT (v. 9)

"For God is my witness, whom I serve with my spirit in the gospel of his Son, that without ceasing I make mention of you always in my prayers."

A. Paul's Redundancy (v. 9b)

"Without ceasing I make mention of you always."

"Without ceasing" is a negative emphasis, and "always" is a positive emphasis. Paul was simply affirming to the Roman believers that he was covering all the bases and praying for them constantly.

B. Paul's Representative (v. 9a)

"For God is my witness."

Since the Roman believers did not know Paul, he called on God to validate his ministry to them. He was saying, "God is my witness, and He knows my heart." Just as God witnessed about Christ's public ministry (cf. Matt. 3:17; 1 John 5:9-11), so also He testified concerning the public ministry of the apostle Paul.

C. Paul's Request (v. 9c)

"In my prayers."

Paul was always in the habit of praying for the saints. He began most of his epistles with an indication of his concerned prayers for the readers. And here he prayed for a group he had never met. He never took for granted their spiritual lives. He never forgot their labor of love, and continued to pray for them.

1. The influence of the early apostles

   a) Acts 6:4—The early apostles said, "We will give ourselves continually to prayer, and to the ministry of the Word."

b) 1 Thessalonians 5:17—Paul said, "Pray without ceasing."

2. The intensity of the apostle Paul

a) Ephesians 6:18—Paul also said we're to be "praying always with all prayer and supplication in the Spirit, and watching thereunto with all perseverance and supplication for all saints." Paul was always praying for everyone.

b) Ephesians 3:14-19—In praying for the Ephesians, Paul said, "For this cause I bow my knees unto the Father of our Lord Jesus Christ, of whom the whole family in heaven and earth is named, that he would grant you, according to the riches of his glory, to be strengthened with might by his Spirit in the inner man; that Christ may dwell in your hearts by faith; that ye, being rooted and grounded in love, may be able to comprehend, with all saints, what is the breadth, and length, and depth, and height, and to know the love of Christ, which passeth knowledge, that ye might be filled with all the fullness of God."

c) Philippians 1:9-11—To the Philippians Paul said, "This I pray, that your love may abound yet more and more in knowledge and in all judgment; that ye may approve things that are excellent; that ye may be sincere and without offense till the day of Christ, being filled with the fruits of righteousness, which are by Jesus Christ, unto the glory and praise of God."

d) Colossians 1:9-12*a*—Paul and his coworkers prayed fervently for the Colossians: "For this cause, we also since the day we heard it, do not cease to pray for you, and to desire that ye might be filled with the knowledge of his will in all wisdom and spiritual understanding; that ye might walk worthy of the Lord unto all pleasing, being fruitful in every good work, and increasing by the knowledge of God; strengthened with all might according to His glorious power, unto all patience and long-suffering with joyfulness; giving thanks unto the Father."

e) 2 Thessalonians 1:11-12*a*—For the Thessalonians they prayed, "That our God would count you worthy of this calling, and fulfill all the good pleasure of His goodness, and the work of faith with power, that the name of our Lord Jesus Christ may be glorified in you, and ye in him."

Paul was consumed with praying for the saints. He endeavored to line up with God's will on their behalf. Paul called on God's omniscience for verification. God, who cannot lie (cf. Heb. 6:18), was Paul's witness that he never stopped praying for the believers he ministered to. He wanted them to know that his failure to visit Rome was not because he lacked the desire, but that it was not God's purpose at that time. Paul's prayers were characteristic of a true servant's heart.

III. A WILLING SPIRIT (v. 10*a*)

"Making request, if by any means now at length I might have a prosperous journey."

A. The Participation

Paul not only prayed for the believers in Rome but also asked God if he might be part of the answer to his prayer. That is a refreshing statement because so many people today want someone else to do the work of the ministry rather than themselves. I have heard people praying, "Lord, raise up someone to reach my neighbor." The real answer to that prayer ought to be the one who prayed it!

B. The Proclamation

Some years ago a film was made called *The Gospel Blimp*. It was about a man who wanted to bring his neighbor to Christ. He went to the extreme of hiring a blimp service to drop gospel tracts in his neighbor's yard. A group of men formed the International Christian Blimp Association to fly over their neighbor's yards depositing tracts. There are many "gospel blimp" Christians in the world. They want to bring their neighbors to Christ, but they won't simply go over to their houses and witness to them.

A man once came to me after our church service and said, "I have a plan to win my neighbors to Christ. And I'd like to know if the church would give me twenty-five thousand dollars to carry out my plan." I said, "What do you need the twenty-five thousand dollars for?" He responded, "I'm going to buy a sophisticated telephone answering system that allows people to call in and hear the gospel. When it's in place, I'll start giving out the phone number to all my neighbors. I won't tell them what the number is for, so they'll think it's for something else. Without knowing it, they'll call and hear the gospel." I said politely, "Sir, you don't need twenty-five thousand dollars from the church. You simply need to go over and tell your neighbors about Christ and what He's done for you."

We don't need gospel blimps or other gimmicks. The key is to want to have a part in answering our own prayers. The prophet Isaiah said, "Here am I. Send me!" (Isa. 6:8, NASB). It becomes so easy to pray for missionaries to reach a lost world, and yet it is so hard to share Christ with our neighbors. If you pray, "Lord, I want this to be done and if need be, I'll do it," then you're showing a willing heart.

Focusing on the Facts

1. Give six reasons that people serve the Lord, and describe the wrong motives behind them (see pp. 66-67).
2. External service is not motivated by a _____ response from the _____ but an _____ response from the _____ (see p. 67).
3. Explain why people struggle with right motives for serving the Lord (see p. 68).
4. Describe three characteristics that show the fervency of Paul's motives (see p. 69)?
5. Why did Paul need to reveal his heart to the Roman believers? Why might they have questions about his ministry (see p. 69)?
6. What is the key phrase in understanding Romans 1:8-16a? Why is it so important (see p. 70)?
7. What is the commonality between serving and worship? Give examples from Scripture (see pp. 71-72).

8. If there's one thing we know about the apostle Paul, it would be that he had a _____ _____ (see p. 72).

9. True or False: A person with a thankful heart recognizes the work of God in the life of someone else (see p. 73).

10. Who was the source of Paul's thankful heart, and who was it mediated by (see pp. 74-75)?

11. What does Paul mean by saying he was thankful for the Romans' faith (see p. 76)?

12. Who did Paul call upon to validate his ministry to the Roman believers? Why did he have to do that (see p. 77)?

13. Describe Paul's prayer life to all the believers he ministered to (see pp. 78-79).

14. Paul's prayers were characteristic of a true _____ _____ (see p. 79).

15. What did Paul's prayer for the Romans consist of? How did he attempt to involve himself in his prayer (see p. 79)?

16. How can you show a willing heart to God (see p. 79)?

Pondering the Principles

1. The apostle Paul had a thankful heart. In almost every one of his epistles, he expressed thanks to God for the ones to whom he wrote. Are you a thankful person? Do you thank God for everything that occurs in your life, no matter what the circumstances may be? Study the following verses and ask God to make you a thankful person: Ephesians 5:20, Philippians 4:6-7, and 1 Thessalonians 5:18. Memorize at least one of them.

2. How often do you pray? When you do pray, how much of that time is spent praying for others? Use the following passages to pray for those to whom you minister, whether it be your family, friends, or those you are discipling or evangelizing: Ephesians 1:16-19, 3:14-21, and Colossians 1:9-13.

3. A willing spirit is a mark of true spiritual service. It is the service that renders not only prayer but also the willingness to be part of the answer. If you pray, "Lord, I want this to be done and if need be, I'll do it," then you're showing a willing heart. Do you desire to be part of the solution in your prayers for others? Do you pray regularly for your neighbors yet remain unwilling to be used by God to reach them? If so, ask God to begin to make

you the solution to your prayers for others. Seek to be "a vessel unto honor, sanctified, and fit for the master's use, and prepared unto every good work" (2 Tim. 2:21).

5
Marks of True Spiritual Service—Part 2

Outline

Introduction

Review
A. Wrong Motives for Serving the Lord
  1. Panic
    a) John 4:23-24
    b) Romans 12:1
  2. Prestige
    a) 1 Corinthians 9:16-17
    b) 2 Corinthians 4:5
    c) 1 Corinthians 9:19
  3. Pride
  4. Peer pressure
  5. Parents
  6. Profit
    a) Acts 20:35
    b) 1 Corinthians 10:24
B. Right Motives for Serving the Lord
I. A Thankful Spirit (v. 8)
II. A Concerned Spirit (v. 9)
III. A Willing Spirit (v. 10*a*)

Lesson
IV. A Submissive Spirit (v. 10*b*)
A. Paul's Commitment
B. Paul's Model
  1. Matthew 26:39
  2. Matthew 6:10

Introduction

In Romans 1:8-16a, the apostle Paul endeavors to open up his heart to the Roman believers. He showed his real motives for serving the Lord Jesus Christ. Other than the Lord Himself, the apostle Paul was probably the greatest servant who ever lived. This portion of Scripture forces Christians who read it today to look inside and see what really motivates them for true spiritual service. It was apparently important for Paul to bare his heart to the Roman believers because he was preparing by the will of God to come to them. He stopped at the very beginning of this epistle—just after introducing the theme of the gospel of God—to show the Romans how much he really cared for their spiritual growth.

Paul had never been to the Roman church, and most of the Christians there had only heard about him. He wanted them to better understand him and his teaching. In verses 8-16, you can see the qualities of Paul's life, the character of his service to Christ, and the motives that moved his heart. In so doing, Christians everywhere can find a pattern for themselves, because all Christians are called to serve Christ. The apostle Paul is an exceptional example of what it means to serve Christ.

Review

A. Wrong Motives for Serving the Lord (see pp. 66-67)

1. Panic (see pp. 66-67)

   Paul wrote to the Romans explaining that his service was not external or legalistic. He served the Lord from the heart.

   a) John 4:23-24—Jesus said, "The hour cometh, and now is, when the true worshippers shall worship the Father in spirit and in truth; for the Father seeketh such to worship him. God is a Spirit; and they that worship him must worship him in spirit and in truth." You cannot worship God with externals, ritual, or routines. You either worship Him from the heart or you do not worship Him at all.

   b) Romans 12:1—Paul said, "I beseech you therefore, brethren, by the mercies of God, that ye present your bodies a living sacrifice, holy, acceptable unto God, which is your reasonable service."

Homeward Bound

There is a story of an old missionary who returned home after many years of sacrificial service in Africa. He was on the same ship with President Teddy Roosevelt. Roosevelt had been in Africa for a big game hunt. When the ship docked in New York, great crowds greeted the President. The press covered it all. The old missionary and his wife walked off the ship unnoticed and made their way all alone to a cheap hotel for the night before traveling West. "It just doesn't seem right," the missionary said to his wife. "We give our lives in Africa to win souls to Christ, and when we arrive home, there's no reward or anyone to meet us. The President shoots some animals and gets a royal welcome." As they were praying before they went to bed, the missionary sensed that the Lord was saying to him, "Do you know why you haven't received your reward yet? Because you're not home." Paul kept that fact in mind. He didn't want to receive superficial or temporal acclaim. He was willing to wait until he went home—his ultimate home—to receive what God had promised him.

2. Prestige (see p. 67)

   a) 1 Corinthians 9:16-17—Paul said, "Though I preach the gospel, I have nothing to glory of; for necessity is laid upon me; yea, woe is unto me, if I preach not the gospel! For if I do this willingly, I have a reward; but if against my will, a dispensation of the gospel is committed unto me."

   b) 2 Corinthians 4:5—Paul said, "We preach not ourselves, but Christ Jesus the Lord, and ourselves your servants for Jesus' sake."

   c) 1 Corinthians 9:19—Paul said, "Though I am free from all men, yet have I made myself servant unto all."

3. Pride (see p. 67)

4. Peer pressure (see p. 67)

5. Parents (see p. 67)

6. Profit (see p. 67)

   It was not Paul's goal to serve the Lord for money.

   a) Acts 20:35—Paul said to the Ephesian elders, "I have shown you all things, how that so laboring ye ought to support the weak, and to remember the words of the Lord Jesus, how he said, It is more blessed to give than to receive."

   b) 1 Corinthians 10:24—Paul said, "Let no man seek his own, but every man another's wealth."

B. Right Motives for Serving the Lord (see pp. 68-72)

I. A THANKFUL SPIRIT (v. 8; see pp. 72-76)

II. A CONCERNED SPIRIT (v. 9; see pp. 77-79)

III. A WILLING SPIRIT (v. 10a; see pp. 79-80)

William Carey, the great missionary to India, had a willing spirit. As he was preparing to leave from England, his friends said, "Are you sure you want to go to India?" Going to India in those days was quite dangerous. Carey was alleged to have said, "I will go down [into the pit], if you will hold the rope" (S. Pearce Carey, *William Carey* [London: Carey Press, 1923], pp. 117-18). That is a willing spirit!

Lesson

IV. A SUBMISSIVE SPIRIT (v. 10b)

"By the will of God to come to you."

A. Paul's Commitment

The apostle Paul did not want to do anything outside the will of God. He began his epistle hoping to visit the Roman Christians if it was God's will and ended it the same way (Rom. 15:32). Paul's life was regulated by a commitment to the will of God.

B. Paul's Model

The Lord Jesus Christ Himself was Paul's ultimate example of One who was committed to do God's will.

1. Matthew 26:39—Jesus said in the Garden of Gethsemane, "O my Father, if it be possible, let this cup pass from me; nevertheless, not as I will, but as thou wilt."

2. Matthew 6:10—Jesus, showing the disciples how to pray, said, "Thy kingdom come. Thy will be done in earth, as it is in heaven."

Paul conformed his life to the will of God. He was utterly concerned with serving Him.

C. Paul's Example

1. Acts 21:13-14—Luke recorded this about believers who tried to dissuade Paul from going to Jerusalem: "Paul answered, What mean ye to weep and to break mine heart? For I am ready, not to be bound only but also to die at Jerusalem for the name of the Lord Jesus. And when he [Paul] would not be persuaded, we ceased, saying, The will of the Lord be done." Paul was being told by everyone that if he went to Jerusalem, he would be bound as a prisoner. But Paul lived for the will of God. And his disciples were resigned to the fact that death might be the will of God for him.

2. James 4:13-15—James said, "Come now, ye that say, to-day or tomorrow we will go into such a city, and continue there a year, and buy and sell, and get gain; whereas ye know not what shall be on the next day. For what is your life? It is even a vapor that appeareth for a little time, and then vanisheth away. For ye ought to say, If the Lord will, we shall live, and do this, or that."

The limiting factor in everyone's decisions should be if it is the will of God. The true servant is totally submissive to God's will. Paul was resigned to God's will, and it didn't matter whether it brought him pain or pleasure. That kind of obedience is not fatalism. Rather, it requires the confidence of knowing that God has the best plan for His children.

Why Pray if God's Going to Do What He Wants to Do Anyway?

Dr. Donald Grey Barnhouse gave a great illustration to convey the relationship between our prayers and God's sovereignty:

"We will suppose the case of a man who loves violin music. He has the means to buy for himself a very fine violin, and he also purchases the very best radio obtainable. He builds a library of the great musical scores, so that he is able to take any piece that is announced on the radio, put it on his music stand and play along with the orchestra.

"The announcer says that Mr. Ormandy and the Philadelphia Orchestra are going to play Beethoven's seventh symphony. The man in his home puts that symphony on his stand and tunes his violin with what he hears coming from the orchestra. The music that comes from the radio we might call foreordained. Ormandy is going to follow the score just as Beethoven wrote it. The man in his living room starts to scratch away at the first violin part. He misses beats, he loses his place and finds it again, he breaks a string, and stops to fix it. The music goes on and on. He finds his place again and plays on after his fashion to the end of the symphony.

"The announcer names the next work that is to be played and the fiddler puts that number on his rack. Day after week after month after year, he finds pleasure in scraping his fiddle along with the violins of the great orchestras. Their music is determined in advance. What he must do is to learn to play in their tempo, in their key, and to follow the score as it's been written in advance. If he decides that he wants to play Yankee Doodle when the orchestra is in the midst of a Brahms number, there's going to be dissonance and discord in the man's house but not in the Academy of Music. After some years of this the man may be a rather creditable violin player and may have learned to submit himself utterly to the scores that are written and follow the program as played. Harmony and joy come from the submission and cooperation.

"So it is with the plan of God. It is rolling toward us unfolding day by day as He has planned it before the foundation of the world. There are those who fight against it and who must ultimately be cast into outer darkness because He will not have in His heaven those who proudly resist Him. This cannot be tolerated any more than the authorities would permit a man to bring his own violin into the Academy of Music and start to play Shostakovich when the program called for Bach. The score of God's plan is set forth in the Bible. In the measure that I learn it, submit myself to it and seek to live in accordance with all that is therein set forth, I shall find myself in joy and in harmony with God and His plans. If I set myself to fight against it, or disagree with that which comes forth, there can be no peace in my heart and life. If in my heart I seek to play a tune that is not a melody the Lord has for me, there will be nothing but dissonance. Prayer is learning to play the same tune that the eternal plan of God calls for and to do that which is in harmony with the will of the Eternal Composer and the Author of all that is true harmony in life and living" (*Expositions of Bible Doctrines Taking the Epistle to the Romans as a Point of Departure*, vol. 1 [Grand Rapids: Eerdmans, 1952], pp. 122-23: used by permission).

V. A LOVING SPIRIT (v. 11)

"I long to see you, that I may impart unto you some spiritual gift, to the end ye may be established."

A. Love Involves Giving

The apostle Paul wanted to give the Roman believers a spiritual gift that would establish or strengthen them in their faith. The primary demonstration of love is giving. John 3:16 says, "God so loved the world, that he gave his only begotten Son." True love always gives. Paul wasn't coming to Rome because he wanted to tour the Appian Way or see the Forum and watch chariot races. He wanted to come because he wanted to give.

Many times in my ministry as a pastor I have thought, *I wonder whether any one is really hearing what I'm saying. I wonder if people really appreciate me or the teaching of the Word.* You can easily fall into a woe-is-me complex. Maybe you've felt the same way in your ministry. If so, you must remember that as long as you look at the ministry you're in as something you give, you will never have that problem. If you look at the ministry as something you get, you will end up with a twisted view of what real ministry is.

1. Colossians 1:27-28—Paul said that "God would make known what is the riches of the glory of this mystery among the Gentiles, which is Christ in you, the hope of glory; whom we preach, warning every man, and teaching every man in all wisdom, that we may present every man perfect in Christ Jesus."

2. Galatians 4:19—Paul agonized over the spiritual state of those to whom he ministered: "My little children, of whom I travail in birth pangs again until Christ be formed in you." I cannot totally identify with Paul, but I have experienced severe pains in my stomach with anx-

iety over the lack of response to the teaching of God's Word. It is as if some people come to church with a thimble's worth of desire for knowledge and spill it on the steps going out.

3. 1 Thessalonians 2:7-8—Paul said, "We were gentle among you, even as a nurse cherisheth her children. So, being affectionately desirous of you, we were willing to have imparted unto you, not the gospel of God only but also our own souls, because ye were dear unto us." No one is more gentle than a nursing mother with her little baby at her breast. The word translated "cherisheth" is a strong term and means "to warm with body heat." Paul was saying, "We provided you with the warmth of our body, as a mother does for her little baby, and we longed for your presence and fellowship."

4. 2 Corinthians 12:15—Paul wrote, "I will very gladly spend and be spent for you; though the more abundantly I love you, the less I be loved." Even if they hated him, he would still love them. The main characteristic of love is unselfish giving.

Look At 1 Corinthians 13

B. Love Involves Giving a Gift

Since one who loves always seeks the best for what he loves, Paul said he longed to impart some spiritual gift to the Roman believers. He wanted them to receive a *charismata*, or gift of grace. Because Paul referred to a spiritual gift—the Greek word *pneumatikon* is used—this grace gift is a gift of the Holy Spirit.

1. Romans 5:15—Paul used the same term to speak of Christ when he said, "Not as the offense, so also is the free gift. For if through the offense of one many are dead, much more the grace of God, and the gift by grace, which is by one man, Jesus Christ, hath abounded unto many."

2. Romans 11:29—Paul referred to God's blessing of Israel when he said, "The gifts and calling of God are without repentance."

Prov. 21:14

3. Romans 12:6—Paul here spoke of the gifts of grace to the body of Christ when he said, "Having then gifts differing according to the grace that is given to us."

The gifts of God's grace are used to speak of Christ, the general blessings that God gives to His people, and of specific spiritual gifts. How is Paul using it in Romans 1:11? I think he is using it in the largest possible sense. Paul may in effect be saying, "For some of you, I'd like you to receive Christ Himself, for others I'd like you to receive the blessings of God, and for still others, I'd like to minister my spiritual gifts among you." What Paul wanted to impart to them wasn't physical but spiritual.

C. Love Involves Giving the Word of God

So much preaching today is superficial. Endeavoring to impart spiritual depth into someone's life is a difficult task. You must build on the foundation of the Word of God. There is no point in giving book reviews or reading emotional stories to my congregation. That would be sheer frivolity. If you love people, you always seek to give them the best you have to offer, and the best thing I can offer is the teaching of the Word of God.

Verse 11 gives us the reason for imparting spiritual gifts: "To the end ye may be established." The Greek word used for "establish" is *stērizō*, which means "to fix," "to confirm," or "to strengthen." Paul expresses the same thought in another way in Ephesians 4:12: "For the perfecting of the saints for the work of ministry for the edifying of the body of Christ." Paul wanted to use the Word of and the gifts of the Spirit to impart spiritual depth in the lives of the believers.

Is Genuine Love Your Goal?

A girl in our church who was a student at a local university said to me, "I learned a great lesson from one of your sermons on love. I always told myself that I loved the little girls in my fourth-grade Sunday school class. They all have small, frilly dresses and the cutest smiles. I told myself I would never miss my class because I love them so much." She went on to say, "One Saturday I was attending a football game at my school—something I do every Saturday—and the Lord convicted me about not adequately preparing my Sunday school lesson. Because I attended the games on Saturday, I was in the habit of running through the lesson early Sunday morning, but it was very shallow and superficial. God pointed out that I didn't really love those girls the way I thought I did because I made no sacrifice in my own life to give them something of eternal value." She ended our conversation by saying, "So from now on, I will not be attending any more football games until my lesson is completed and I feel I can impart to them something of eternal value."

VI. A HUMBLE SPIRIT (v. 12)

"That is, that I may be comforted together with you by the mutual faith both of you and me."

A. Mutual Benefit

Paul was not coming in as the spiritual expert to dispense information to the Roman believers. He wanted also to be encouraged by their faith. That is a demonstration of his humility.

There are many people who think they have much to give and nothing to learn. A true servant of God should never feel superior to others. Paul was saying, "I am going to minister to you and impart my spiritual gift, but I know in return that you will minister to me as well."

John Calvin once wrote, "Note how modestly he expresses what he feels by not refusing to seek strengthening from inexperienced beginners. He means what he says, too, for there is none so void of gifts in the Church of Christ who cannot in some measure contribute to our spiritual progress. Ill will and pride, however, prevent our deriving such benefit from one another" (*The Epistle of Paul the Apostle to the Romans and to the Thessalonians* [Grand Rapids: Eerdmans, 1960], p. 24). Paul was eager to learn from inexperienced beginners.

B. Mutual Blessing

New Christians have come to me and said, "I don't know why I'm talking to you. I know there must be important people for you to talk to. I know you must be busy. I'm just a nobody." They think they have nothing to offer, but according to verse 12, the great apostle Paul himself was willing to learn from the most inexperienced of believers.

I had dinner not long ago with someone who kept saying, "I am so sorry for taking up your time. You're probably not interested in speaking to me." I kept saying, "Wait a minute! I appreciate your talking to me. This is building my faith, and I'm having a wonderful time." I don't want people to deny me that privilege!

The humble teacher says, "Let's learn together." One writer said humility is that low sweet root from which all heavenly virtues shoot. There are few things worse than a pompous teacher who treats you as if you knew nothing and he knew everything.

1. 1 Peter 5:2-6—Peter directed this comment toward elders: "Feed the flock of God which is among you, taking the oversight of it, not by constraint but willingly; not for filthy lucre but of a ready mind; neither as being lords over God's heritage, but being examples to the flock. And when the chief Shepherd shall appear, ye shall receive a crown of glory that fadeth not away. In like manner, ye younger, submit yourselves unto the elder. Yea, all of you be subject one to one another, and be clothed with humility; for God resisteth the proud, and giveth grace to the humble. Humble yourselves, therefore, under the mighty hand of God, that he may exalt you in due time."

2. Philippians 2:3-5—Paul said, "Let nothing be done through strife or vainglory, but in lowliness of mind let each esteem others better than themselves. Look not every man on his own things, but every man also on the things of others. Let this mind be in you, which was also in Christ Jesus."

Conclusion

The true servant of God is always thankful. He's always prayerful because he knows that although he can thank God for what has been done, there is still much that needs to be done. And, he's willing to be the solution to the problem if it's God's will. He seeks to give to others, not only for what he can give but also for what he can receive.

Someone once wrote the following about a willingness to serve (cited in A. Naismith's *1200 Notes, Quotes and Anecdotes* [Chicago: Moody, 1962], p. 179):

> I gave my service, but with a heavy heart,
> And with it went but little love or trust:
> He was my master, I must serve or die,
> So I gave my service for I must:—is the
> voice of destiny.
>
> Then, o'er the dreary dullness of my road
> There came the kindling ray of better thought:
> I owed my service to a loving God,
> So I gave my service, for I ought:—is the
> voice of duty.
>
> And lo! the Master made my service sweet,
> And, like a ray of glory from above,
> There came the knowledge that to serve was joy,
> And so I give my service, for I love:—is the
> voice of devotion.

Focusing on the Facts

1. Why was it important for Paul to reveal his heart to the Roman believers (see p. 84)?
2. How did Paul show the Roman Christians that he cared for them (see p. 84)?
3. What can Christians gain from reading Romans 1:8-16 (see pp. 84-85)?

4. The apostle Paul did not want to do anything outside the _____ of God (see p. 87).

5. Who was Paul's model for pursuing the will of God? Support your answer with Scripture (see pp. 87-88).

6. True or False: The limiting factor in everyone's decisions should be if it is the will of God (see p. 88).

7. What is the relationship between a Christian's prayers and God's sovereignty (see pp. 88-89)?

8. Why did the apostle Paul want to come to Rome (see p. 90)?

9. The primary demonstration of love is _____ (see p. 90).

10. What did Paul mean by saying he wanted to impart a spiritual gift to the Roman believers (see p. 91)?

11. What is the best thing a pastor can offer his congregation (see p. 92)?

12. What was the purpose in imparting spiritual gifts among the church at Rome (see p. 92)?

13. How did Paul demonstrate a humble spirit in writing to the believers in Rome (see p. 93)?

14. True or False: A true servant of God should feel superior to others (see p. 93).

15. What did John Calvin say about learning from others (see p. 93)?

16. Summarize what a true servant of God is like (see p. 94).

Pondering the Principles

1. True spiritual service is marked by a submissive spirit. The apostle Paul would not take one step further unless he knew it was the will of God. Is your life marked by a submissive spirit? Do you endeavor to live each day in the perfect will of God? Study the following verses and let them be a model for how you conduct your daily affairs: Acts 18:21, 1 Corinthians 4:19, and James 4:13-15.

2. The true servant of God is marked by a loving spirit. We should seek to give more than receive and to build up others in the faith. Paul wanted desperately to exercise his spiritual gifts among the Roman believers. How desperately do you want to use your spiritual gifts to minister to others? Read the following verses and ask God to give you the same desire: 2 Corinthians 9:14, and Philippians 1:8, 2:25-27, and 4:1.

3. Humility is an important mark of true spiritual service. Humility does not involve thinking lowly about yourself; it is not thinking about yourself at all! Do you possess a humble spirit? Do you become jealous when someone else gets the credit you think you deserve? Do you receive an equal amount of joy when others are blessed? Over the next few days, memorize Philippians 2:3-5, and ask God to make you a humble person.

6
Marks of True Spiritual Service—Part 3

Outline

Introduction
A. The Touch Up
B. The Testimony

Review
  I. A Thankful Spirit (v. 8)
 II. A Concerned Spirit (v. 9)
III. A Willing Spirit (v. 10*a*)
 IV. A Submissive Spirit (v. 10*b*)
  V. A Loving Spirit (v. 11)
 VI. A Humble Spirit (v. 12)

Lesson
VII. A Fruitful Spirit (v. 13)
    A. The Purpose of Ministry
    B. The Pressure of Ministry
        1. The emphasis (v. 13*a*)
        2. The examination (v. 13*b*)
            a) Attitudes
            b) Action
                (1) Romans 6:22
                (2) Philippians 4:17
            c) Addition
                (1) Romans 16:5
                (2) 1 Corinthians 9:22
    C. The Pleasure of Ministry
VIII. An Obedient Spirit (v. 14)
    A. The Obligation to God (v. 14*a*)
        1. The compulsion
        2. The commitment

Introduction

A. The Touch Up

It is said the artist Hofmann would periodically visit the
Royal Gallery of Dresden, where many of his greatest
works were displayed. He would come with his paints
and brushes and spend many days touching up his mas-
terpieces to make them look their best. That is what the
Master Artist—the Lord Jesus Christ—desires to do with
His children. The picture is already painted; it just needs
a small touch up now and then. As we go through life, it
is easy for some spots on the canvas to fade. In studying
Romans 1:8-16*a*, we may expect the Lord to touch up
some of the faded areas in our lives.

B. The Testimony

In Romans 1:8-16*a*, the apostle Paul opens his heart and
reveals the motivation for his ministry to the Roman
church. There would be no better way for the Romans to
get to know Paul, since they had never met him, than to
hear of the man behind the message. He did not begin
sharing his theology, doctrine, convictions, goals, or purposes. First he shared his heart.

I had the privilege of attending seminary to study for the ministry. I learned much from the books I read, the notes I took, and the papers I wrote, but I learned far more from the lives of the men who taught me. Rather than focusing on what they said, I concentrated on why they said it. That is what Paul did with the Romans. He in effect said, "Before I give you my theology, let me give you myself." Paul is a model for all who serve Christ.

Review

I. A THANKFUL SPIRIT (v. 8; see pp. 72-76)

II. A CONCERNED SPIRIT (v. 9; see pp. 77-79)

III. A WILLING SPIRIT (v. 10a; see pp. 79-80)

IV. A SUBMISSIVE SPIRIT (v. 10b; see pp. 87-90)

V. A LOVING SPIRIT (v. 11; see pp. 90-93)

VI. A HUMBLE SPIRIT (v. 12; see pp. 93-94)

Lesson

VII. A FRUITFUL SPIRIT (v. 13)

"Now I would not have you ignorant, brethren, that oftentimes I purposed to come unto you (but was prevented thus far,) that I might have some fruit among you also, even as among other Gentiles."

A. The Purpose of Ministry

Paul saw the ministry as a quest for spiritual fruit. He saw it not as an end in itself but as a means to an end. The purpose of ministry is not the ministry itself but the fruit that results in people's lives. The quest for spiritual fruit was the mainspring of all apostolic activity. Jesus said,

"Ye have not chosen me, but I have chosen you, and ordained you, that ye should go and bring forth fruit" (John
5:16).

*Look:
John 15:1-17*

B. The Pressure of Ministry

A person who serves with his whole heart is content only
with spiritual fruit. Some people are content only with
prestige, acceptance, or money. The devil tries to put that
thought into my mind sometimes. Sometimes thoughts
like these pop into my mind: *What do I care about people? I
know I'm saved and going to heaven. I'm well paid. At the
worst, I've got a good job with a lot of security. I can't lose.* But
that is Satan's lie. You can let him pressure you to settle
for less than God's best. When Satan plants a thought like
that I remember that I am not content to simply be taken
care of or appreciated—the only thing that makes me
happy in the ministry is bearing fruit. Second Timothy 2:6
says, "The farmer that laboreth must be first partaker of
the fruits."

1. The emphasis (v. 13a)

"I would not have you ignorant, brethren."

Paul used that phrase many times for emphasis. It
points to an essential truth that Paul wanted to get
across to his readers. He used it when he talked about
the doctrine of salvation (2 Cor. 1:8), Satan (2 Cor.
2:11), the second coming of Christ (1 Thess. 4:13), and
spiritual gifts (1 Cor. 12:1). Paul was saying here, "I
desperately wanted to come to you that I might bear
some fruit among you." You can measure your commitment to Christ by whether you are more concerned
with what happens in others' lives than you are with
what happens in your own.

2. The examination (v. 13b)

"I purposed to come unto you (but was prevented
thus far,) that I might have some fruit among you."

*Attitudes
Action
addition*

What kind of fruit was Paul speaking of? Three things
are spoken of as fruit in Scripture:

102

a) Attitudes

Galatians 5:22-23 says, "The fruit of the Spirit is love, joy, peace, long-suffering, gentleness, goodness, faith, meekness, self-control." Paul wanted to come to the Romans with the right attitude.

b) Action

Fruit is not only who you are but what you do.

(1) Romans 6:22—Paul said, "Being made free from sin, and become servants to God, ye have your fruit unto holiness." Paul is saying that forgiveness should usher itself into holy living.

(2) Philippians 4:17—Paul said, "I desire fruit that may abound to your account." Because he was such a model for the Roman believers, Paul wanted to bear fruit among them. But he also wanted to see them respond with the right attitudes and actions.

c) Addition

Paul wanted to bear some fruit among the Gentiles, and in so doing wanted them also to share Christ with others.

(1) Romans 16:5—Paul referred to converts as fruit: "Greet my well-beloved Epaenetus, who is the first fruits of Asia unto Christ." The concept of fruit is applied to people who come to know Jesus Christ and are added to the Body of Christ. Paul desired for men to be saved.

(2) 1 Corinthians 9:22—Paul said, "I am made all things to all men, that I might by all means save some."

Paul's desire was to see believers display right attitudes and actions. He also wanted people added to the kingdom. The latter is the thrust of verse 13.

When Paul finally did arrive in Rome, his desire was fulfilled, for Philippians 4:22 says, "All the saints greet you, chiefly they that are of Caesar's household." He had been used of God to win people in Caesar's household to Christ. His was the ministry of bearing fruit.

C. The Pleasure of Ministry

I could not survive a ministry of maintenance. To be satisfied with having a group of sanctified saints sitting around looking at each other is not real ministry. You must see fruit in the lives of those you touch. That is the joy of service. I become excited after hearing many testimonies of how God has changed people's lives from the teaching of His Word.

The world is in a state of confusion and chaos from all the lies, wrong answers, and opinions. My wife and I walked into a store and overheard two of the employees talking about the book of Genesis. One man said, "Of course, everyone knows that Genesis is only a fairy tale." The other man agreed. The first man continued, "Genesis is meant to teach us a mystical moral." My wife spoke up and said that's foolishness. She's right. That incident simply points to the folly of the world. Crashing into the world and bringing the truth is what real ministry is all about.

VIII. AN OBEDIENT SPIRIT (v. 14)

"I am debtor both to the Greeks and to the barbarians; both to the wise and to the unwise."

A. The Obligation to God (v. 14a)

"I am debtor."

For the apostle Paul, ministry was not an option; it was an obligation. He did not make the decision for ministry on a whim. He did not one day say, "Let's see, I could be a tentmaker, or possibly an attorney, or even a politician. No, I think I'll become a preacher." The apostle Paul owed a debt to God.

1. The compulsion

   Paul said, "For though I preach the gospel, I have nothing to glory of; for necessity is laid upon me; yea, woe is unto me, if I preach not the gospel! For if I do this thing willingly, I have a reward; but if against my will, a dispensation of the gospel is committed unto me" (1 Cor. 9:16-17). Paul didn't want anyone to name a city after him or erect a statue in his honor. He knew he owed a tremendous debt to God because he was killing Christians until God turned him around and called him into the ministry. Paul knew that had God not intervened, he would have continued to kill Christians. Paul was saying, "Don't commend me; I have a debt to pay. God brought this to pass."

2. The commitment

   A young man asked what motivates me to study week after week after week. I said there are times when some passages are so exhilarating, I can't wait to get to Sunday to preach. But there are other times when I battle time problems and priorities that crowd out my study time. The ministry doesn't seem that exciting then. I really have to fight my way through those times because I know I have a debt to God. If you are involved in Christian service only when you feel like doing it, you haven't learned the kind of service that Paul described here. In the midst of a tough time in ministering to people, sometimes all you can rely on is your obligation to God.

B. The Obligation to Man (v. 14*b*)

"I am debtor both to the Greeks and to the barbarians; both to the wise and to the unwise."

The implication of verse 14 is that the debt Paul spoke about is a debt *to* God *toward* the Greeks and barbarians. Because of the ministry God gave Paul, he was obligated to serve men. If I am walking down the street and pass a house on fire, and the family inside is unaware of the situation, I have an obligation to help them. I cannot stand on the curb and think, *I wonder if they're worth saving.* Because they are in a dire situation and because I have the information that can save their lives, I have an obligation to them.

If a man crosses my path who is in need of clothes or food, yet I say to him, "Be warmed and filled," in the spirit of James 2:16, I have not discharged my debt. Paul owed the Gentile world the truth because they were on their way to hell, and he knew the way to heaven. Jesus said, "Unto whomsoever much is given, of him shall much be required" (Luke 12:48). The apostle Paul had an obligation—first to God and second to the Greeks and barbarians.

C. The Origin of the Terms

"Greeks and barbarians . . . wise and unwise" are parallel phrases. Paul was speaking of the educated and uneducated. The Greeks were sophisticated and thought theirs the most elite culture around. When a person spoke a language other than Greek, the Greeks thought their unintelligible chatter sounded like "bar-bar-bar-bar." Thus, foreigners became known as barbarians. They were regarded as uncultured, uneducated, and unintelligent.

Paul knew he had the same responsibility to the educated Greeks as well as to the uneducated barbarians. There is a subtle point here: you cannot pick and choose to whom you will preach the gospel. Every so often I will hear someone say, "I'm trying to reach the elite." I say, "Why? Are the elite better than the rest?"

1. Acts 10:34—Peter said, "God is no respecter of persons." And Paul endeavored to reach all people for Christ, regardless of their race, background, or financial status.

2. John 4—The first person Jesus revealed His messianic identity to was a half-breed Samaritan who had a handful of husbands and was living with a man who was not her husband (vv. 16-18). The gospel is the great equalizer because it does not differentiate

106

between persons. She could be saved just as anyone could. It is easy to be trapped into being a respecter of persons. Many tend to evangelize high-income people and pass by lower-income people. However, the poor are more open to the gospel than the rich because of their needs.

IX. AN EAGER SPIRIT (v. 15)

"So, as much as in me is, I am ready to preach the gospel to you that are at Rome also."

That wonderfully balances fulfilling your obligation to the Lord. We are to be happy and eager to fulfill the responsibility God has committed to your care.

A. Paul's Eager Spirit

Paul was consumed with doing the work of the ministry.

1. Acts 20:22-24—"I go bound in the spirit unto Jerusalem, not knowing the things that shall befall me there, except that the Holy Spirit witnesseth in every city, saying that bonds and afflictions await me. But none of these things move me, neither count I my life dear unto myself, so that I might finish my course with joy, and the ministry, which I have received of the Lord Jesus, to testify the gospel of the grace of God." Paul's self-preservation was not at the top of his priority list. His main concern was to fulfill the plan of God and the ministry God had given him.

2. Philippians 1:21—"To me to live is Christ, to die is gain."

3. 2 Corinthians 5:8—"We are confident, I say, and willing rather to be absent from the body, and to be present with the Lord."

4. Colossians 1:23-24—"I, Paul, am made a minister. Who now rejoice in my sufferings for you."

5. Philippians 2:17—"If I be offered upon the sacrifice and service of your faith, I joy, and rejoice with you

all." Paul in effect was saying, "If I lose my life reaching you for Christ, that would bring me great joy."

Paul's own personal life was never the issue. Life had only one purpose for him and that was doing the will of God. He was always eager to preach.

B. Epaphroditus's Eager Spirit

In speaking of Epaphroditus, who had the same desire, Paul said, "He was sick near unto death, but God had mercy on him; and not on him only but on me also, lest I should have sorrow upon sorrow. . . . For the work of Christ, he was near unto death, not regarding his life, to supply your lack of service toward me" (Phil. 2:27, 30). Paul explained that God was merciful in preserving Epaphroditus because both their hearts would have been broken had he not been involved in ministry.

Paul was so eager—like a racehorse in the gate or a sprinter in the blocks—waiting to gain the victory. Because Paul was like that, God had to hold him back once in a while because he was so ready to go. Are you as eager? Is that the kind of service you render, or does someone have to prod you along with all their might just to get you involved? If your service to Christ comes from your whole heart, then you will be eager.

X. A BOLD SPIRIT (v. 16a)

"For I am not ashamed of the gospel of Christ."

A. The Antagonism

It is commendable that Paul was so eager to go to Rome because he knew what a volatile place Rome was. The citizens of Rome were heavily involved in emperor worship and overt paganism. It was likely they would despise the gospel of Jesus Christ. Nevertheless Paul was not ashamed of the gospel of Christ. When Paul had the opportunity to preach, he preached to anyone.

When people are unashamed, they can do amazing things. Those who are ashamed might be eager at first, but when the battle starts, they faint. They are what I call "sign-up specialists": they sign up for almost everything the church has to offer and then drop out because of their lack of commitment. Eagerness needs to be followed up with boldness.

B. The Attitude

The pagans in Rome had branded Christianity as atheism and cannibalism. In their lack of understanding about the Christian communion service, they assumed Christians ate one another. The Jews had branded Christianity as heresy, blasphemy, and lawlessness. The gospel has always been a stumbling block and a rock of offense (1 Pet. 2:8). However, Paul didn't care. He was not ashamed of the gospel and was bold enough to preach the gospel message to anyone. He proved that in Jerusalem, in Athens, and would prove it in Rome as well. He proved it in every city he visited because the servant of the Lord should always go into any situation with an unashamed, bold attitude.

Commentator Geoffrey Wilson wrote, "The unpopularity of a crucified Christ has prompted many to present a message which is more palatable to the unbeliever, but the removal of the offense of the cross always renders it ineffective [Gal 5:11]. An inoffensive gospel is also an inoperative gospel. Thus Christianity is wounded most in the house of its friends" (*Romans: A Digest of Reformed Comment* [Carlisle, Pa.: Banner of Truth, 1976], p. 24). Many have emasculated the gospel so that it won't offend anyone.

I spoke at a youth rally on the need to be saved. After my message, the wife of the rally director said, "Your message offended me because you preached as if all of these young people were evil." I said, "I'm glad you heard that message because that's exactly what I wanted to communicate." She said, "But you turned them off." Sadly, that is the predominate mentality of many people today: they don't want to offend anyone, so they compromise the message. However, those who stick to the real message of the gospel are unashamed in their boldness in speaking about Christ.

C. The Action

I am convinced that the church of Jesus Christ has not even begun to see what God can do in our world if we began to live out all ten marks of true spiritual service. The world would be forever touched if believers served out of thankful, concerned, willing, submissive, loving, humble, fruitful, obedient, eager, and bold spirits. However, the tendency is the opposite. Ask God to prevent you from becoming comfortable in your Christian life or spiritually lazy. Ask Him to make you a true spiritual servant.

Focusing on the Facts

1. Why would the Lord want to touch up the canvas of our spiritual lives (cf. Rom. 1:8-16a; see p. 100)?
2. In Romans 1:8-16a, the apostle Paul opens his heart and reveals the _____ for his ministry to the Roman church (see p. 100).
3. True or False: Studying what a person says is always more important than what his life is like (see p. 101).
4. How did Paul see the ministry (see p. 101)?
5. The purpose of ministry is not the ministry itself but the _____ that results in _____ _____ (see p. 101).
6. What was the mainspring of all apostolic activity (see p. 101)?
7. True or False: A person who serves with his whole heart is content only with spiritual fruit (see p. 102).
8. How can you measure your commitment to Christ (see p. 102)?
9. What three things are spoken of as fruit in Scripture (see p. 103)?
10. List the nine attitudes described as fruit of the Spirit (Gal. 5:22-23; see p. 103).
11. Give scriptural examples of the fruit of addition (see p. 103).
12. With which concept of fruit is Paul mainly dealing in Romans 1:13 (see p. 104)?
13. Explain the eighth mark of true spiritual service (see p. 104).
14. What is meant by having an obligation for ministry (see pp. 104-5)?
15. What was the debt Paul owed to the Gentiles? What was his message to them (see p. 106)?

16. What was the difference between the Greeks and the barbarians (see p. 106)?
17. Explain the ninth mark of true spiritual service (see p. 107).
18. What was Paul's chief concern in life? What was low on his priority list (see p. 108)?
19. Why was it a commendable thing that Paul desired to go to Rome (see p. 108)?
20. Who are the "sign-up specialists" (see p. 109)?
21. The servant of the Lord should always go into any situation with an _____, _____ _____ (see p. 109).
22. What is a predominate mentality of many people today concerning the gospel and its presentation (see p. 109)?
23. What qualities could Christians adopt to change the world for Jesus Christ (see p. 110)?

Pondering the Principles

1. The apostle Paul longed to bear fruit among the believers in Rome. He wanted to have the right attitude toward them, take the right course of action in furthering their spiritual growth, and desired the salvation of all those he came in contact with. Do you possess a fruitful spirit? Do you have a good attitude toward those with whom you come in contact? Are you endeavoring to bring others to Christ? Review pages 102-4; then take the following passages and determine which could be classified as attitude, action, or addition fruit: John 4:35-36, 12:24, Colossians 1:3-6, or Philippians 1:9-11. Once you've determined which fruit is being talked about, ask God to allow you to have a fruitful spirit.

2. No matter what the cost, Paul was consumed with doing the work of the ministry. His personal welfare was not his main priority. Life for Paul had only one focus and that was the souls of lost men and women. What is your preoccupation? Is your heart consumed with doing the work of the ministry? Study the following verses and ask God to cause you to have the same kind of attitude toward the work of the ministry: Isaiah 6:8, Matthew 9:37-38, and Acts 21:13. Memorize at least one of them.

Scripture Index